JOURNEY TO THE INNER LIGHT

JOURNEY TO THE INNER LIGHT

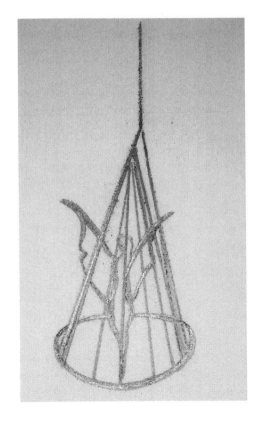

LISA ALEXANDER

ISBN: 0692450149
ISBN 13: 9780692450147
Library of Congress Control Number: 2015907980
Lisa Alexander, Hollis, NY

TABLE OF CONTENTS

ACKNOWLEDGEMENTS

Acknowledgments and dedication to:

My family, Son Richard, friends, and Claude Saccaro
Dr. Leon Perkal, Professor Yearwood, Professor Archer Irby,
Professor London, Dean Timothy Taylor, Dr. Aliza Holtz.

SON

To my son, Richard Andre Mark Lalanne
Most special one indeed,
This bodily angel came to life through me,
He is my song, given as the greatest offering from above.
This wondrous child that came from light is of godliness and purity.
He is as pure as the holy one Himself.
The great one dwells within from the day he came to be
The spirit of the light shines through him
He brings forth beauty from the day the angels lifted his face to the almighty to be kissed
He touched his mind and hands with the gift of music, a stroke of genius once again from the most high
My child, in you, He has placed the soul of the prince of peace who has dominion over all kings and princes.
That light that you experience from young is His, touching your soul.
As you were born, angels danced merrily about your head.
They too knew that you were special and wanted to feel their master's power through you.
As you ignite with the God of light you become one.
You say the force of the light is no longer—
My child, it is not true, for the force is all around you, He is with you for all time.
You are his forever, and the dark ones are envious of this.
They fail to realize that you are untouchable, for you are His creature, His work, His joy.
He touched you with His music from the time you were in the womb.
No one can ever comprehend the connection that you and He have.
He has knighted you as one of His own, as a prince of kindness with a heart and soul that is pure.

No darkness or man can ever touch what God has created—
You are a part of his covenant, an angel, and God is calling you for a greater purpose in life.
No harm comes to those whom God holds dear; you are forever in His presence, untainted, untouched, and pure as the heavens above,
And that, any man on earth will envy.
My son, my love, heaven is with you, they protect you.
You are that bodily angel that God has touched—your mind, soul, and spirit
It is up to you to let Him in completely
God is showering you with blessings, and no one can break His bond.
We won't let them!
So let us both rejoice in our father's name forever.

ENTRAPPED

Why do you hold your love entrapped in a cup?
Why not let the cup spillover, as though it were a stream or a waterfall;
Flowing freely over glistening edges of rocks that shimmer when sunlight reflects upon them,
Or when two lovers' bodies are encompassed, and their kindred spirits are merged into gentle passionate embraces?
In you, the brightest of light comes from within, like that of natural things in their surroundings
Ah, such beauty you emit from your very touch, words, and spirit.
Be free, I say, being free, like the lovebird singing their song in the open skies; until the clouds absorb their tune and it reaches heaven.
Let the cup spill over; allow your love to emerge from within and be born anew.

UNYIELDING

There it goes again, that ringing in my head. Like a sound of a banshee crying out to be free, your siren is ongoing and relentless to my very core.

If I could forget this name, I would rip it savagely from my chest so that I shall not dwell or linger in this pain no longer.

Impossible you are.

The turmoil of you is in my soul like a dark stormy night where God exerts his power and thrashes his hands across the still waters.

Like Him, such power you possess over me!

How painful and unyielding you can be when you speak the words that are so empty.

Why is it that you are comparable to stone and dead like the bark of a rotted tree?

For someone like you, who can possess my very being and render me powerless, it is mundane.

I cannot fathom the thought of such mastery. It is your ongoing torment that convolutes my thoughts and weakens me.

These images of you and me won't let me alone.

But on the other hand, perhaps, just perhaps it is of relevance that my life's joy, which continues to be intangible, is my destiny.

This wonderful and remarkable joy brings forth such pleasure, a journey that has yet to be unraveled, but a thirst to know more of the mind, heart, and spirit—

For his name will remain branded on my heart for all time.

You know your name.

My love, you are well worth it, the pain, the torment, and your sharp tongue I gladly welcome.

by Sky Simple Man

STOICISM

Father tells me, Be still my child and watch the works from above, for everything happens in due time, and this time no man has yet to comprehend the miracles that await you.

All that you want, I already know; I feel your pain; I know your heart and your love.

Have patience, child, have patience of a mother who has been waiting many hours to bear her first child.

Plant roots of stoicism in thyself.

The works at hand will be so swift that they will go unnoticed by any man but be witnessed by the heavens above.

FULL, NOT EMPTY

I am not empty, I am full.
Much of life's course has yet to be completed.
There are those who think they know my inner being but know me not in the least.
It is only life's pain that dwells within and knows me best;
It builds and builds in my chest as a tower in the sky. Once an empty tower, its space is now filled with heaven's clouds,
For the course of this life has been conducted by the ones that have sought to eradicate this light within,
But little do they know that there is only one who has that privilege, and it is the creator.
Only He knows all of me.
It is that being that my destiny has manifested. From him these words are from purity and beauty,
Not man.
For every void that is within me is now full, completed by the Creator who rules over all things.

THE EYES

Some say the eyes are the windows of the soul.

I say, at times, the eyes that you look into could be unfeeling and cold like a glacier.

The sharpness of the eyes can pierce your flesh like a warrior whose skin has been punctured in battle,

But behind them one can read and see many things.

They tell a story of sorrow, pain, happiness, and love.

The eyes speak truth that can sometimes be concealed;

They have something deeper to express, yet they do not want to reveal it.

Through the eyes, some disguise their intent as good, but in reality it is falseness with a dark agenda through these eyes.

Supposedly this window of the soul tells all of oneself, but sometimes behind them they are deceptive, lifeless, containing nothing.

These eyes emit imaginings in the mind that send messages of fantasy to human thought,

They conjure up feelings where we wish these visions could be but will never be.

These eyes are also connected to the thought, heart, and soul—

If not of kindred spirit, it will leave the viewer helpless, hopeless, yearning for a want that will never manifest,

For even the eyes cannot force what will or can't be.

Only nature and the universe control such things that are from the eye to the heart.

There are times when the eyes are like a veil, and the smiles are really grimaces, not of the pure earth with unclean thoughts.

All around us are the eyes of contempt, none are containing angelic souls.

Then what do you do when you can't read through the window of the soul?

7

It is only love that shines through that is pure; the power is so great that it breaks down the coldest of eyes, which are truly the windows of the soul

SIGNS

Are there signs that go unnoticed?

Are there tiny miracles around us revealing the meaning of life?

Does one look for signs of goodness in objects and numbers or natural occurrences?

We are told from the most high that man's number is 6 and that His number is 7.

But the dark one, we know his numbers; it is not worth mentioning, though through this darkness, the creator made light, which is truth.

But if numbers represent something, does everyone have their own number?

If so what does it mean to them?

Where does it fit in their life?

Is it of relevance?

No one knows, but it could be that everyone is given that number as a reminder of something larger in life.

We may be given this special number from above, somehow to be imprinted within us from the day we begin to the day we are no longer.

When we go to our father's home, this is when we will begin to understand our mere existence.

CONNECTION

Is it feared to make the wrong choice, like driving down a one-way street toward traffic?

Blatantly, a companion on two occasions strolls down to the very place where one really belongs. If the chosen path was taken and given by God, which direction should one follow?

Physicians may analyze and question God's work, but He will leave many dumbfounded each time they see His creation.

Many a time the viewers are learned from books and think that they veer in and anticipate the future of their prey,

Protected by one who moves too close for comfort's sake or for the wrong reasons

The connection is not there, and the fiend is only said to leave one alone but continues to make his whereabouts known in the shadows, lurking and stalking like a slithery serpent; using others to carry out his actions to hold you for their own benefit.

For if there were a connection, one would just be true and befriend, not look to unclean thoughts and move on to the next.

It is God who connects people, not man.

Start over and be not of a brute that controlled in B.C. but act of the current day, when people are allowed to make their own decisions,

For forced behavior only brings forth pain and hurt.

It is not of the natural world, and there is no connection when God is not involved.

IMPRISONED

Eyes looking out beyond these cold bars of entrapment:
Is it of mind and thought that holds one back for the thirst of what is?
Does one not want to swim in the stream of what some say is ecstasy?
Why does one hold oneself inside, like oxygen waiting to be exhaled?
Why dwell inside one self so long? Is it to avoid the desire to feel all that
is beautiful in life?
As the sun catches images of the human form and casts back shadows,
so do the eyes; they reflect to the mind what could be, as one watches
life.
But if such offerings of life are of falseness, then one should not go beyond those cold bars; nevertheless, the choice is to remain imprisoned
within them.

TRUTH

What is truth? Is it words spoken from the holiest of books? Or is it a true love that once was, but is now left brokenhearted?

Could it be the journey that man has trodden down his weary road? Down this road his quest is to look for truth.

Is it the scientist who discovers a cure? Or is it the knowledge learned from a scholar?

Preeminently, truth is truth. The word truth is a derivation of Him. That is true.

It is neither scholar, man, scientist nor the like, but the almighty Himself. He is truth.

HEART ON THE SLEEVE

My friend, you are the truest of all friends, you know my heart as well as I know yours
You say you wear your heart on your sleeve? Indeed it is true

You are like the gentlest of soul's that ever was
As you cried on my shoulder that day it was as though an angel's tears fell from your eyes and kissed my shoulders
I felt so honored in that very moment that I was blessed to have your soul pour out
This is when we became one in spirit
For that day locked us together as friends for all time
But as one great one said to me, your tears were not in vain, as I assured you on that day
For the Gates of heaven blessings were on their way!
They sent you the most divine angel of all angels, your personal gift to have, hold and cherish forever
Your wife is your gift those tears were tears of sorrow because your tears were for tomorrow
The tears you have are not of pain but of joy in life that comes thereafter
My friend, you are forever my friend.
Remember, God blesses you because you wear your heart on your sleeve!
Happy Birthday Jay!

CONTRADICT LIFE

One word from his lips said to me, Happiness, but from that word derives love.
How can one tell what is in the soul?
My love, you know me all so well,
For those moments stolen were not for any other but you.
They were not promised to the falsehood of life's acts; as such acts are rehearsed in a play,
But the very lesson taught is now gone to waste.
Your essence is spent with companions not of kindred spirit, for your wisdom of pure thought and heart once held the keys to this open door.
My love, remember the day of your truest of words?
So why now do you contradict life?

A PARADISE

Alone is how we come into the world, but many feel that alone we are
just self-absorbed.
Some live through their material gains and objects.
Souls that are empty vessels reveal no difference than the bark of a hol-
lowed tree;
This is how the heart that lacks the spirit needs to draw Him in.
Otherwise, one is left befogged and in a daze because of life's miseries.
But fret not, says He, "You are never alone when you put your faith in
me,"
For our only misery is that void of light that we need to draw near until
one day, when we are taken hold by the sands of time, gradually misery
no longer exists for you or me.
A place that is unlike the earth, never heard of,
A paradise where complete compassion that is filled with intoxicating
love for all.

RETURNED THROUGH GRACE

Nearing the darkest hour in life, love prevailed.

Spirits welcomed me in a time when twilights were coming to an end;

In that very moment, when the lights grew dim, the touch from a lover's hand quickened me,

Tears were gently wiped away until every element of anguish disappeared,

Pain ceased to exist and was obliterated by this Godly creature.

As this angel lay beside me, he whispered in my ear, "Not yet. There is more to see, more to touch, more to feel, and more to love."

Indeed, I thought this gentle creature's word of omniscience was spoken from the soul of the most high.

It was from this angel's lips to my ears, and in that moment in time, it served as testimony that all spirits were not only in our thoughts but also in our hearts.

As the spirits pranced freely around this portal of light, I clearly understood that this was man's soul lifted for that one woman who danced the dance in a time that was dark. She was obviated, released, and freed. No other one than an angel could possess such miracles of absolute tranquility; love prevailed in the darkest hour of twilight's culmination.

ALL

Appear and disappear like a dream…
Did we have it all?
Planned to observe the actions of two, formulated to conspire like science projects.
Oh, but whatever the project, let me be there again, let them witness the manifestations of kindred spirits formed from above.
The power in your wondrous eyes lights up heaven's doorways.
So gentle is the smile that you can charm the most menacing of men; your tongue utter words that pour out like the fragrance of honeysuckles.
How sweet but dangerously poetic! Why is this earthly creature residing here in this space and time?
Why aren't you up above, dancing among the angels?
Nonetheless, one shan't question the Almighty's work. Though His work may be simple, it is by far complex in the making of you.
Miraculously, He made day and night; however, gloriously He plucked your spirit from the night and the day.
From what one can see, you possess two sides—day and night.
You disappear and reappear like misty rain in early morn when the sun has burned it away.
Remember, there'll be a day when you will come again, but in the dream state where all things are possible.
All and all, sometimes we fall deeply.

ALPHA

One has belonged to you since the beginning of time.
Just as one was formed in the womb, God placed your name in the mind as the first thought.
In the heart's pulsation, the first feeling commenced, signifying resplendent love;
Out of the womb, a light was immersed and glorified the vessel
The great one then touched my lips and formed from the mouth my first cry, which was the utterance of your name.
At that very moment, the majestic one aligned the stars in the universe and raised a soul up to unite with its kindred
Bestowed on two; now they are locked in time, where the alpha creates a cycle endlessly in both the past and the afterlife.

AWAIT

You thirst. Drink here, my child, for I will surely quench your every desire if you just put your trust in me.

Believe in me, I am your Father of fathers. Look in no other direction but here; the strong builder never buckles in the spirit.

One from above says, "I am the doctrine engraved in tablets that Moses held. Know my thoughts and do my will. Listen and hear the complete truth told before time."

The voice speaking inside is your intuition.

The same truths have been here from times past and present.

Nature and human nature are all one; man is eminently designed to bring things anew and not for spoil, for the offerings of the world are but empty shallow showcases, a facade of material objects in the world; one can't and will not be fulfilled.

Only the word should one seek; listen to the voice in the mind beckoning to your woes.

Wisdom spills from within and transforms into elixir that restores life. Be not attentive to the matters of the day; utter words to consecrate your belief in me.

There is no other way but the spirit.

Rejoice in my name and discover an inner strength, for I am your true love and self-doubt is not warranted in my presence.

My child, countless wonders await you in dark times when you can't see clearly the plan that is unfolding, as it will be a plan naturally given as blessings from up above.

AWAKENING

The highest element in life is love.
But what is higher than love?
I say it is more powerful than love, and it is He who graces us with His presence that is greater.
He is the creator of divine and infinite love and all things surrounding it, the major difference in man's love and the great one's is that His is unconditional.
No man can reach such heights of unadulterated bliss— except through the Holy Spirit.
What is better in life than to dwell in our majesty's house, where we find eternal peace within our spirits?
For the prince of peace resides in this chest endlessly. The spark is that light carving the soul, like chiseling wood to create. We are also clay, fashioned after this great love that He pours into every man or woman. Oh how immeasurable is the power of the Miraculous One to move all things of the earth to His liking.
Once again, He has captivated this great soul and intertwined His thought and words in the mind, body, and soul. I've evolved into His very being.
I have become of sound mind, and I will look to the Father to guide my steps to anew. His sacred garment conceals me; His great arms comfort me, protect me, and strengthen my tormented heart.
I am forever dedicated to our Father in all that I do. I will rejoice in His name.

> My father, my prince, my intimate one, you are everything. Without you, I am nothing. I thank you for showing me infinite, true, and unconditional love that I can count on.

Oh glorious one! I give of myself openly as you have sacrificed all for my salvation.

BALANCE

Bound together by the spirit, time is but a minor factor when it involves love,
Patience is worth all restoration when destinies are entwined,
Impossible happenings are not enigmas for the Great One to handle.
Thoughts are gathered collectively to set life in motion, for the troubles faced are but the hardships of yesterday, and a rendering of miracles clears the path and brings about resonance within.
The Great One grounded the spirit like roots in the earth; stabilizing all acts.
Captivated minds are no longer under control, but are in optimal equilibrium, for mind and spirit become one.
The universe spews out the wonders all about those who kneel down to pray, and the secret ones are selected to manifest all things that appear surreal.
Astonished by our faith, our Father whispers extraordinary blessings;
He proudly reveals that His love and ours are bound by the spirit,
He finds those whom He loves and challenges them until they grow ever so magnanimous. Not only has He articulated His children's minds, but He cleverly placed the spirit of David to create a lion's heart. In the hearts of the few, the soul of God is the truest link to unconditional love for honoring Him.

BLACK WOMAN

Like a starry night up above, a crown of grace lies atop our head.

Soul warriors of the night are kneeling down, giving praise with all heart's despair and plight. Tears from yesterday give new sight.

When a black woman tomorrow succumbs to nothing but sorrow, behind her tears she'll find inner light.

For the many who see this gentle creature—and though her skin is dark, one should not remark, for her life's meaning is misunderstood—the story goes beyond today and tomorrow, but the questions are answered in yesteryear.

The melanin in her DNA is a miracle. Some may see the color as hideous, but in God's eyes, this creation is stupendous.

But the Great One covered these beauties with the color of soil, representing a metaphor of nurture and nature.

Our skin may be dark like the night, but it is in our eyes where the bright stars of the heaven's skies linger with just a gentle touch; it was from His finger.

Nevertheless, more work has transformed black women into many colors of the rainbow—now called multicultural—with their amazing glow.

Why that is natural?

But ah, the beauty of the black woman's soul has risen like that of the sunrise from yesteryear's defeat until victory rings true for another day.

We are like bonds that are unbreakable with knowledge, wisdom, and power that are unspeakable beauty in the soul.

How astonishing that our spirits unfold! Many a time the world stomps us down, we still emerge like birds and take flight.

A black woman will never retreat, for she knows life is but bittersweet with all her might.

For her, challenges begin the transformation of a new being,

Because all of the world will stand back and start seeing.

So, black woman, embrace the universe below and above, while the world looks up to see a great crown of jewels placed. How great is the world when you're seen with grace! Your majesty gives His honor to be worn by incredible black woman.

A SHOWERING OF PRAISE

Power is what God breathes into man and all things around from the very soil under our feet to the skies above. It is his doing.

A few miracles are phenomenal evidence of His majestic power. The fluidity of rivers and their movement downstream emits electricity.

Everything has its purpose, man's labor, too, has a part in His plans; from the beginning of time until now, He joins together the blessed ones.

He shows His gratitude by graciously showering gifts from His house, As we thank Him, He bestows mere excellence in a craft or talent placed in all to use to praise Him continuously.

BOY OF WOOD

What moves in the stillness of objects?

Imagination and creativity come like child's play, for questioning ones ponder the mind and tinker about like fragmented mechanical apparatus given way to automation; such objects are no longer operable.

Nevertheless, parts that are inanimate work with screws and rivets excluding automation, like that of the wooden boy, from an old man's fantasy.

Which brings me to wonder, was Pinocchio built with a soul? Then how would he know what is truth or fabrication if made from wood? Surely his master created him imperfectly hoping to find some humanness dwelling within. In desperate need of a son, he too wanted to fill a void.

It was only his nose that gave away his misdeeds; imagine many who are like him:

Hypothetically, many of us would be eyeless; resembling Cyclops monstrosity of what is man

Subtle, insidious, and cumulative effect to bring about a cause to act—

Was something read long ago within the construction of the strand?

Oh, nothing but the highest of adoration for the Maker. Among us dwell many Pinocchio's', imperfectly stupendous in heart.

AS HE IS REINCARNATED

Evolved from a cocoon, high in the grandest of trees, metamorphosis begins once spring has sprung. Beneath the skeleton and tissue a wing has formed.

How beautifully and gently the outstretched wings meet with the breath of life: air. As the butterfly takes flight, he is lifted with the air and breaks free from the cocoon.

Fragments of the cocoon float downward to the ground, disintegrating into the earth.

Full of amazement, eyes before Him reveal this tiny creature, an acknowledgment of God's magnificence displays a rainbow within those very tiny wings.

With just a touch of the Great One's hands, the rainbow is replicated with an array of colors, but from the sky's colorful ceiling.

He is now in the kingdom of unfamiliar creatures that dwell like him.

The butterfly jumps with glee and joy, shouting; "Now I'm off with His breath as my wind to find a gentle mate;"Or the butterfly will arrive too late, 'twas his fate on this very day. It is not miraculous to you or me that reincarnation is a possibility.

CANCER

The growth inside became a living creature that metastasized.
Many may find the name to be ghastly, exuding fear. With it comes the face of death and darkness.
It is actually a stage that brings forth a transformation, stripping down the exterior shell, but ah, the interior grows inwardly fiercely in spirit as the millions of hairs numbered on one's head fall, it is but a trillion times more brilliant to come.
Some say, "Oh my God not the C word," and they think this is the end—but nay, 'tis not the end but the beginning, a rebirthing coming not from thy mother's womb but through the womb of the light.
Cancer came with the dark, the light took over.
Chemo and radiation cannot control the manifestation, for it is God's work.
The path opens up a circle or whirlwind that magnifies the soul.
Awaken from this somber sleep, my child. There is work to be done— by my hand and not man's.
Biologically I have fashioned you, your mother was the vessel that bore you. Your physical self is in a fight with the spiritual self in my realm, I see. I created and know all.
Each cell that lies beneath has purposefully begun to poison the form in order to be reborn.
For all things are controlled by me—the metastasis that fired up was put out by the light placed in your core, so the fight of the cancer was at war with me, and I am your eyes, ears, thoughts, and wisdom.
Never will I forsake you; the cancer was placed to bring about a splendid you
My love, my own, and for my child; says He from above

CHAMBERS WITH PURPOSE

This cavity encloses the mystery and the workings of the most inventive feat ever. The heart is what we call it, but it serves more than just the biological function.

It protects as a barrier and a doorway between you and the world.

Like the heart, the mind holds thoughts in its cranial cavity where one can envision places never seen in the waking world, but in the mind one can invent or create one's own world.

Many ponder the makings of the mind; significantly, the mind and the heart are entwined intricately. Both are equal in their purpose: to sustain and embrace life.

Miraculously, the elixir or hemoglobin prolongs these magnificent instrumental givers of life

The heart alone supplies the elixir and its electrifying biological functions in the anatomy, but it also has multifaceted purposes like emotion, desire, pain, pleasure, and compassion.

The fourth chamber of construction is one of the true works of art, for no man can replicate fully the heart and the quintessential representation it embodies.

It is exquisitely defined and connected with the mind and soul yet more involved than we can ever know or really understand.

Simply, the four chambers of the heart spell out the essence of the word LOVE

The L in one chamber has a specific meaning that can be applied to life; the O is the second chamber with the purpose of optimism; the V is the third chamber for virtue; the E is the fourth for exquisite. This chamber is intricately designed by the One who loves infinitely.

Ultimately, the definition stands, longing, offering, victorious for all eternity, as true as the heart and mind,

CHAMPION OF CHARACTER

Virtuous one has long before left an imprint in the mind;

Enticement of the human tongue grows ever so weary with a creature of God;

Influences from the dark ones concur to find flaw in one who is led by the inner voice, and human nature gives way to those who are weak in the word.

Circumstances are forced to test the threshold to question if one is true. Accidental happenings are no mistake in His world and eyes, for his spirit world has created something additional to the creature that man loathes—controversy raises God's name as the praises are lifted high as one kneels down to him.

Observing behavioral patterns is not scientific but is an act of Him telling the soul to look His way, for in history man has practiced in these ways before.

Father says, "I know all, my child; I see all, for I am the creator of humans, human nature, and all things upon this earth;

There are no mistakes or accidents in the heart that one or many can hold back one's destiny

Shield yourself through me; I am your buckler and your shield like that of a warrior

Essentially, I sent forth my very own for your salvation so do not fear.

So within all who believe, I have placed in you the Champion of Character, human nature, neither scientist nor scholars can performs such acts, it is I and only I," says He from above.

CHANCE

Gratitude extended to all the educators and mentors for all that has empowered one; many steps are from the originator

The sharpened mind is your keen abilities in the making; wonderment has created a being that thirsts for knowledge evermore.

Pain and suffering illuminate where a burning desire seeks for scholarly status

One looks up to you like mountainous regions standing firmly on the ground—proud, unstoppable, unmovable, and graciously imprinting a lasting effect that's profound—

Encircling and drinking in knowledge all around, honorably delighted to have been your student, learned ones revealing the great of the greats.

Introductions are necessary and so is pain in order to grow

Nevertheless, slowly, not to make haste, absorb like a babe to a suckling

Evolve, become a new creature to spring up like the seed you planted.

It was you, the educators and mentors, who planted the seeds of growth in the mind

Though at times it may not be revealed, you are forever in my heart, in remembrance for the place I will always admire forever.

CHOSEN WORDS THROUGH ROCK

Mountains and words are strangely connected; metaphorically both are derived from similar origins.

However, mountains are carved by nature's evolution while the mind is cleaved from the thoughts of a higher being.

A mountain's peak is sharp and can pierce like the negative utterance of words. The wrong words can pierce the heart like daggers of sharp tips of a mountains peak.

Visually, mountains can elicit charm with the array of colors as the sun sets behind them. Like the words, it too can elicit charm; as a correlation, both are equally connected in harm as well.

Similarly, the mountain's surface could be smooth like words.

Some mountains' texture can be rocky—chiseled and cracked—

Words too can produce a texture that is metaphorically disempowering within their negative intent

It is important to choose the words that can build like a mountain and from words that rise like the morning sun.

CLOUD

Clear sky, the truest of aquamarine blue, there are no clouds visible.
Strangely, oracular phenomena and manifestations occur.
The sky takes on life of its own; it isn't lightning, thunder, or rain.
Suddenly, clouds—dark, grayer than steel and iron—sheath like gun metal wrenched not from this earth. Hands form terrifying and shockingly in appearance, almost like a terrestrial. Terrifying clouds form; phalanges appear with a striking resemblance to human hands that surrounds this prodigious creature. Blackness creeps as if night falls without stars
How it lashes against the windows while many lie asleep; there is only one to witness its angst.
It strikes violently, unlike any other natural thing from above or on earth.
Who can explain this occurrence? Is this a message sent for all to take heed?
As it continues to lash at the window, as quickly as it appears, it disappears, dissolving into clear calming water as if it were rain, and why unbeknownst to mankind something is left unexplained once again.

COERCION

Disjointed elements and forms of persuasion, carbon copies all about to
force uncanny behavior slightly resembling scorn and grimaces—
No light dwells in an empty vessel.
Love thyself immensely, then one does not need to gravitate to forms;
be gentle and open the mind and pure heart.
Manifestations of the true destinies are drawn like magnetism,
Hypocrisy does not exist among distasteful acts.
Create a prison or dungeon of ill-mannered thoughts of fantasy.
Why waste precious energy negatively?
Unnatural things are not of godly presence; however, nature has its op-
posite force, where negative meets positive.

CONTINUITY

What is the mystery?
Why ponder the natural flow in life?
Everything around us is created by the Excellent One.
When we cease to exist, the cycle of life continues—
The earth is our being, fertilizing and giving life to future generations.
Gravestones are not the end; the soil enriches the earth to bring about
new life, fruit bears on trees to cultivate flowers and all other living
things.
Restoration has come since the beginning of time and has been a part
of the plan, and continuity is the main scheme of things, for all living
things within space are connected for all time.

CROSSING

Once we have crossed, there is no return;
We become addicted to our Father's light.
The quest has become just as significant as water and air
Some say, a closed one cannot enter—this very statement here may be
true; nonetheless, it is in its own right fraudulent, for our Father can
open even the heart that has been soldered together like molten steel.
His great might can open anything with just a light thrust,
The soul is the gateway, and the door can only open to those who are
from the likeness of Him.
It is never forced, for such quandaries are not kindred in the least.
The pureness of the light guides one to the crossing, and in this great
quest, not only do we find ourselves, we embark on the covenant of the
purest of pure.
Our Holy One lights up any man's darkest of hours time after time.
The crossing is preeminent to our existence. This is where we find the
bridge is drawing closer to the soul.

CULTURES BANKRUPTED

Such robbery as the banks of souls empty out like banks of money floating on a river, each bill symbolizes an infinite soul that once was before corruption.

Man continues to consume and live materialistically—there is no purpose to such an empty existence.

Look how man travels back and forth in search of the unknown through possessing objects, dwelling in worldly things that contain nothing of significance, lacking substance.

Why bear witness that the money represents man's greed?

They are but a lost flock that has gone adrift.

Our Father of Israel does not want man to beckon to such a lame existence. He wants us to praise him. He is calling his flock one by one, and all those that believe in Him, He never gives up on.

He puts into our hearts hopes and dreams, not despair, for the souls that have been robbed will be restored and become full henceforth.

The banks that are the house of the Great Spirit will hold Him who dwells within.

There are many multitudes and cultures floating on the banks' river; nonetheless, at the end, He will be there to greet those who believe in Him and bring hope to all.

DEAF AND ASLEEP

One is numb and mute to wants and desires as words are conjured up in the mind and formed on the lips. Are they true?

Some words fall down to the earth like solid stone, forming tombs, dead tones, without expressions and feelings, deep inside the sleep.

One need is to be awake where the heart beats immensely; nonetheless, one whisper from my love's voice and this sullen state emerges.

The vessel is stirred up like the whirlwinds from a frigid winter's day, and thereafter a lasting effect of warmness takes over.

Limpness and motionlessness have given way to the spirit that is freed and united with love again:

It is a resurrection caused by this angelic creature where one is entranced again.

But wait! It is not real, only manifestations of thoughts playing over in the mind—

How glum, and how morose the heart has sunk deeper into its cavity, back where it belongs—in deafness and sleep, in a silent world without the One.

DÉCOLLETÉ

Reduction thrives to hierarchy levels, but in spirit—
Being of lowly feeble states drives one toward faith, and despair births
humble and honorable greatness.
Loyalty is proof to the Majestic One like His crown of highness—
Forever He is watching the activity of the heart's authenticity.
Rest yourself in the highest hierarchy above, not in the worldly; there-
fore, find yourself low and not in the surroundings of mediocrity.
Keep all dwellings pure and simplistic, allow no room for doubt.

DEDICATION

Look inside this door to the heart and notice the soul seeking the devotion from above.

Why spend time on worldly occurrences, when one can swim in the lake of something greater?

Follow the footsteps leading to the true power of love.

In the mind's eye, the echoing of past, present, and future is but chaos. Nevertheless, the Majestic One eats away at cancerous disarrays where the substance lacks enlightenment, He sets the path straight where it once was uncertain, and a worship of thankfulness is all He asks.

In such prayers, one feels a powerful connection and belonging; all torment, turmoil, and pain is eradicated and lives only in temporary spaces and time.

All are saved by his glorification and mercy

In desperation, many invite him through the open door to take full control. In his hands

We are like clay, molded to withstand all trials and tribulations, but he lets us know we must learn to endure all the shortcomings in life as He sacrificed Himself for many to follow in truth.

Consequently, many or a few give very little of our time in honoring him, and when we do, it is but a selfish act, not praying just because we love Him,

For artifice is not what He wants; it is our genuine love and devotion.

DEEMED IN THIS LIFE OF FRENZY

The anticipation is but a farce. Realization sets in and plays no part of the past, present, or future.

Occurrences are not coincidental; nonetheless, they are planned beforehand for many to view, mumbles, mockery, and idle chatter for passersby to hear—

Did you spread your want through the universe? Aren't there any good Samaritans left?

Bitterness is coming from the empty void that cannot be filled. Have your life on a stage for everyone to view.

Have you not found someone to fill your void? Is paper supposed to buy the soul and spirit?

Intentional roadblocks are placed forced connections with strangers, ridiculed and nullified actions—and for what? It was never concern for another, but only for you—

The mental state is challenged, and this very being knows the puzzlement bestowed.

You state care, love, and marriage—what hypocrisy! It is grotesquely dark and not from the light to take part in suffering.

Is this tormenting a part of the universe's payment in full? Why, many sit by and watch like a play in a theater. One says, "A leopard doesn't change its spots." How clever, how cliché.

Many ponder or inquire about a mind that is but a mystery—

Only He above knows all of you. As always, man is perplexed about life's happenings and while scientists work their magic, their hypothesis fails again.

Man is unpredictable, and the spirit cannot be broken, especially one of God's creatures. The human heart is impenetrable. Once it is full, there is no hope for change
How perplexed can an emotion be?
For the audience observes a fallen one deemed in this life of frenzy.

DELUSION

Build your life piece by piece with brick, straw, and mortar. Unspeakable power from above is watchful with the happenings.

In the mind, pawns on a chessboard represent souls moved for checkmate, gone down spiraling into the underworld. Chances come and wither away in the wind.

Machinations left up to the doer and watchers waiting to see one fall. Gone down to nothing? They say it is better to be nothing in the eyes of man.

Success means different things to others—materialism—but success could mean simplicity to a few.

Nevertheless, something in the eyes of God knows all these things during the making, and His eyes are never in displeasure while looking inside your soul to see His face.

Why play? He tells His creatures, "Be true, courageous, and fearlessly fierce with my power. Don't convolute your mind or crowd it up with delusion placed before you by the world.

DEVIATION

While sitting on a commuter train, a regular day-to-day activity.
Thoughts ponder through the mind endlessly—
Past eccentricities of life have controlled one's mere existence.
One shudders as if chilled to the bone, for the fabric of this life is mayhem interwoven in other beings' lives. Was it a time of truth and dare?
Unfolding before one's eyes are contours of the familiar forms that move around in past, present, and future—
Found in strange embraces and stolen kisses gone to waste.
Was it all child's play, like a game of Monopoly?
As history is in the making, some may have been light, and others are heavy like charred metal scrapped from a junkyard of confiscated vehicles.
A risk taken, but was it worth it?
Dim nights with glistening candles, topped with whipped cream amid sensual desserts again. Was it worth it?
Such bittersweet mysteries give one the chaos again, where the heart lingers and is left to its own vulnerabilities.
This is the day when a train ride has one pondering the footsteps of lives past, revealing deviation from the true path that still waits.

DISAPPOINTED AND AWAKENED THROUGH PEN AND PAPER

Conceal, block, and push away. Have your innocence stolen so young. Inner voice speaks—trusts in no man.

Are the signs so unnatural to force an ungodly one to observe?

How many years must one wait to get a turn? What for the flesh? There is so much more beneath the skin. The skin is just a layer; consequently, words and talks of the flesh are but superficial chatter, for the learned gain their knowledge from books, but true life is learned firsthand through experience

Godly ones do not behave in this manner—they are the intelligent ones.

How can one enter another's world when one has yet to know or understand? And is not invited

Only the spirits intertwine that illuminates holds the key to the true heart

When passions, feelings, and spirits unknown to your world are from pure souls, they are not tainted. They repel like magnets—opposite forces, no apologies. The soul is not for you—not of this time nor space. Why ponder about the outer appearance and the flesh? Waste no one's time and move on to your next form that welcomes such displeasure.

Knowledgeable ones explore life's mysteries with a pen, as most writers do; such writers release their inner emotions by pouring them out onto paper, for the magic is in the pen, and this is when the fantasies come to life.

Why, the words dance on the paper and unfold before you!

Your mind fires up such life, and now you've got it—you have found your spirit poured out on the page.

Why waste one's time on hate and a wanting that will never manifest? This emotion is but a grotesque characteristic for anyone to portray.

With your pen, you can have anyone you want and have your way; you can empower yourself with words, and no one can take that—it is your sword.

Inscribe on your paper your purest of genuine desires, not greed and lusts.

Unfortunately, this emotion is distasteful and unappealing

For the pen and the paper are true lovers—interlocked, concealing, blocking—where one does not push away, so empower and create your world to please your wants.

Nevertheless, one will always be welcomed into the world through ink and paper where one has ultimate control without blocking, concealing, or pushing away.

DISCOVER

Discover yourself like an unopened door that has never been walked through. Inside ourselves, we hold a mystery.

Looking at the outer exterior we are just flesh and bones, for the Holy God uniquely crafted the mind as though He were sharpening each brain cell with a metal tool.

But the tool is His spirit's formation within. There is much more to just the form when constructing great minds.

He that is all knowing captivates His creatures by embodying the light. Through life's journey and happenings, coincidence is merely a farce—Outside forces from the universe create a doorway of mysticism; the unknown awaits and delves deep into the soul to bring out the heart.

DREAMS

Dreams are the interpretations of life. In them, they bring forth the deepest of human thoughts and feelings.

Sometimes these dreams light a path for a new direction; they act as a compass, like that of a sea captain navigating his ship.

So many times dreams have brought about creativity, allowing the mind to soar where the heart desires.

Why, you can create your own universe or world, for these dreams are powerful tools of divine inner light, energy; they are mystical in themselves, crafted by the Great One.

Messages are but premonitions disclosed in the mind's eye—in dreams, they are powerful phenomena where visions are manifested in man's soul.

Images in dreams become a part of the unconscious mind doing things unimaginable.

Each night, your mind creates a world that is surreal; you can be on another planet or in spirit realm.

Nonetheless, oracle intervention is most powerful. The Infinite One reaches through portals to search your soul. In dreams, His face is reflected in your heart.

In your love's mind, He touches the vision with His fingertips to majestically emit light.

Sparks emerge, giving way to enlightenment that produces illumination strikingly resembling the world of superb love.

How wondrous is the world of dreamers, where the Master holds the ultimate keys to ecstasy combined with the soul.

DUBIOUS

Side effects, actions, and responses rendered. Look through the fog. Is something out there?

The character is tried once more and up for debate.

Eventful clever planning gives way to fear or faith. Who will listen to sullen cries in the night?

Man?

Scientists study men and mice. Behavior is not peculiar to you nor me.

Careful not to tread too close to those you love. That is not permitted.

One is programmed to rethink and do the unthinkable—

While kneeling down, eyes closed, the heart cries for Him in every way like the very air has been removed.

Irrational behavior is love; oh no, this is far from being a farce. It is the human heart created by the Wondrous One.

Dubious minds act, ponder, and plan out what is to be, and the Maker of all thoughts creates meaningful acts.

Benevolent characters exhibit distinctive qualities.

This is His way to the soul.

EIGHTH

Extraction is to bring about abstraction.
Here in this life there is distraction,
For many seek to find satisfaction
Beyond the eighth is where the mystery lies. Long ago, the spirit from the past has empowered the inner being to not lose.
Victorious as the Great One, who takes in all, for his power is attraction,
For love is the ultimate manifestation,
The eighth is the course and final destination.
World views and paths have distinctly taken a new direction;
Separated from the original force, one is drawn in unification.
Spirits concealed like a veil and then lifted to uncover the truth that was forbidden.
Opposites blocked—one lost, one found. Has the material world taken the soul?
Eighth as reminder of a sacramental offering to never forget that
In this life, there is no time to regret.
Alignment of the light is directed back to its origin, the eighth.

EMOTIONAL BLACKMAIL

Disarrayed and in a world of emptiness, a wanting from the heart renders one vulnerable in every waking hour.

Emotions run to the very pit or core like a rind eaten from a melon.

Sunken eyes from rain that falls on a pillow—

Why some stand by and ridicule the angst that one feels

Left behind on purpose, without a choice, but premeditated.

For those who watch, are their expressions filled with wry amusement?

Oh pain, how great you are in this chest.

Pleasingly, while viewers watch with glee, the inclination is mine, and I am happy to entertain you, for the pain I gladly welcome—at least that part of me is real, and you are not.

If only you knew of such distress, you'd accept that a heart like mine is asunder and can be mended back to life.

It is he that is more powerful than any other, where all things are possible and —one does not dare question, so bring on your emotional blackmail, for it is but a mere folly on your part as such action persists. It is of mundane nature, irreconcilable differences, and it pierces the heart.

Sadly, it is the envious ones who lack the emotion to ever be in the shoes of those who are emotionally blackmailed.

EPIPHANY, PART I

The moment the great book opens, sparks flicker, ignited into an eternal flame, blinding the mind's eye, preventing darkness.

For without light, wisdom and knowledge cease to exist.

Infinity has struck and aligned one's course back to its origin.

A repetitious act or is it epiphany? A path a thousand times more brilliant from Him, a manifestation and understanding neither you nor I can really comprehend.

The course of the mind to the great fortress is indeed blocked from the Divine.

Oh great book! How you've quickened the soul to take flight and broken strong holds of the imagination.

Grab hold! For this journey is for the swift and the mighty of men.

Barricades are demolished with just a rumble from up above; encroaching no longer exists in this time or universe. All are set free!

Occurrences unheard of, words of knowledge are restored; every moment is blissful.

Belonging has found her way back to our king of kings.

EPIPHANY, PART II

A great phenomenon has come from beyond and with it births insight unearthly, exquisitely stemmed from the womb that weaved another—
Oracle has sewn it shut; an opening unfolds to that of a kindred state
Authenticity allows for no other false processes, ousting all of what contains artifice
Or is it motive that drives deep into the mind's eye, evoking reaction.
Constantly drilling toward the knowledge of the soul's thirst— to get to the core;
Seek the pure quenching that is left by a hunger that is satisfied.
Without this fulfillment, torment and tantalizing of the spirit reaches for more.
Oh, give in to…what is there to surrender?
Did Shakespeare surrender all in the matter of splendor or an unopened door of enchantment never tasted? Calamity or tragedy, life is sweet in the bitterness of desire.
Why let the mysteries conjure up unseemliness, for many lie awake to grab onto and hold the absolute.
No other than scientific laws of nature emerge or philosophical notions subdue ambiguous chatter.
All about one is noise, the world is filled with it; the Great One seeks the quiet.
Go back to the start whence one has been drawn from the stars, the great universe before time was time; epiphany has chosen its spawn to grab hold of.
So do not concern oneself with the dwelling of the form epiphany is your full.

EVE

Overwhelmingly free in the likeness of Him—
If prophesized, then why is the clamoring of others force to surface from many directions?
The house of many houses continues to make for an understanding that is yet and still a mystery for you and me; the power unheard of strives in an existence that is not justified for all to bear witness.
Loved and in want of? In fact, one can question, or read it in books, or look into another's soul.
The weakness of the spirit is tested by many, a parade of nays and yeas to give a nod of acceptance, to be free and roam the earth, to see the true believers. Father has done this many times ago—
Only—and only if it be true—what does it mean to many or some?
Who can tell one of true faith? Is it found in the great houses? Or does it linger in the vessel itself?
To be in the arms of another is but a farce if this supposedly the way to define the self.
Freedom comes in the way of the spirit that sprouts wings to take flight.
Pictures in the mind of oneness is lewd and stemmed from the Garden of Eden
Did it really start from Eve?
Unappealingly ignorant to state that Eve is to blame; why, she is the mother of mothers, in fact, the first. Oh, but the serpent glided down the tree to greet and entice this wondrous creature, Eve.
For what would've become of the world if she'd not bitten that apple?

Existentialism on Eve's part, not knowing what was considered good or evil, naïve was she to have taken that bite with her childlike inquisitive nature.

The fruit called to her, the slithery serpent aided the process and advantageously coaxed Eve with this object.

This aspect juxtaposes with that of the Little Red Riding Hood, in that the serpent and the witch are one in the same,

Foreshadowing the aftermath of disasters that lie ahead, mystery in the sweetness of unfolding and giving birth to the world of many nations came from Eve's lips.

For the fruit is highly significant and the test of man's temptation—

Why, without that first taste, we wouldn't have known the world as it is today or yesterday. Existing would have only been Adam and his Eve,

Why, how convoluted and chaotic the world must be, it is known with that great act; there would be no you nor I, great feats would not have been conquered; many who are joined with great causes would never fight with the spirit of patriotism for the greatness of people, country, or purpose.

Father must have known the mischief of His children, as He made them with His mighty hand.

Like the Eden of yesterday and many of today, even where there is beauty lays deceit. But Eve did not deceive; she was one who made it possible for all mothers to conceive—

Inexplicably brilliant,   the master plan for all of mankind to aim toward coexisting harmoniously.

FACES

Empty expressions with the absence of light; reflections of ghosts past,
present, and future—
Bitterness of parched lips, a show of no compassion, utilizes the flesh as
a meal in search of contentment.
How unappetizing are we of little faith?
Look into my face and find the mirror image of yourself,
For I am the way where your soul will be released and returned to light
This is when your face will once again resume all the presence—
Angst and torment can no longer linger—
A peace will consume your inner being and raise you up toward glory
and grace.

FOREIGN

Pulled out of the flesh, a foreign toxic attack that turns any man or woman's world upside down,

The invader is unmasked, revealing itself as an arch nemesis to engulf the flesh like a macrophage eliminating unwanted debris.

But the enemy implants itself and takes on new life as if it belongs, tearing down every natural part of God's creation, rendering one vulnerable as it becomes a part of the deoxyribonucleic acid structure.

Replication is what it lives for; it is utterly destructive, finding new ways to optimize its existence,

It destroys and diminishes lives, leaving families fatherless, motherless, and childless, slowly breaking down what many built in a lifetime

If one survives this great and horrific ordeal, then they're a winner. But still, is one the same?

It deteriorates the flesh like piranhas gnawing on shark remains.

This great evil is the enemy to us all and must be ousted forever.

FREE

Alone is how we come to this earth; however, it is with the light of God that we are truly free.

Many believe that owning possessions and acquiring material gain is the source of freedoms.

Nay, that rings false, for the richest of all are those who are pure in spirit.

For that reason only, one is truly empowered and free.

Those who rely on material to fill the void are reluctant to find what is true from above; such beings souls are drifting into a fog that never clears in early morn.

Chained misery locks these lonely hearts into despair, seeking solace; something with substance and meaning is missing within the soul.

One foot is in the grave. But in the mind's eye, many should look to search within—forget materialism. We should soar freely through the soul and the mind's eye to witness our Father's power.

Leave the acquired possessions behind, for one can't live or leave this earth with them.

GIFTS FROM GOD

Men say you can't achieve your goals without a foundation built early in life; I say God's given spirit within is a natural gift.

It is not man who decides such doctrines or policies for the destinies of greatness or born in the light of a woman's womb.

It is the light that stimulates articulation in the mind. This is where creativity, knowledge, and wisdom come about—

The fountain of life commences beyond the world but in Divine manifestations, and miracles around you are lifting up the spirit and embracing the stream of gold inside.

Even a man who is impoverished is drawn toward the Great One's face to thank him for the chosen gifts.

No room is left for pity, for sacrificing the soul for God is truly a blessing.

When man strips your very being to leave you naked, the world wants a taste, for God is the truest pioneer of the spirit of man—He created it.

Mysteriously, He weaves a plan that gives birth to inner strength when you listen to His voice, which is the soul.

He is hope and opens doorways to opportunities where gifts are exposed to make monumental differences.

GREAT MIND

A great mind is His, grounding your feet.

Hold your position and obey, I command you! Humble yourself with grace and words of wisdom.

Virtues, secretly spoken into the mind, flourish with Thy gifts bestowed that none can take away.

"Use the hands to make what pleases me, for all that I manifest through you is for a better way. Look hither to this light as I touch your mind, neither forget your heart, for mine is in yours."

All things are not lost, but the path will restore you once again—no bother to those who mock what they do not understand.

"A long time ago, they did not take the time to praise me as the faithful ones do by keeping my name and devoted love. Never will I turn away nor forsake my child whom I love."

GREATNESS

On the contrary, collapsing effortlessly, floating as if walking on air, wandering the earth again, soaring over the snowy Alps and mountainous terrains—

Choice and voice in unison; swirling around in the cold winter's air, hiking to reach the peak of the mind's eternal bliss—

A great light, blinding to the human eye, leads the way amid the navigation that failed. How long can we depend on mechanical devices?

Left to walk aimlessly until footprints are left in the snow, within the tracks lies the mystery. Perplexed about the sound in your head?

Are you really? Intuition is clarity that leads you to the doorway of the soul again, revisited and called upon to bring out that hidden darkness to reach the Divine light.

Claim no other—to be caged is like being an angel that has clipped wings.

Searching for the mirrored image, lost in the wilderness, a familiar voice calls from inside, destined to higher plateaus of the earth, where man finds the challenges of nature's cold breath: the wind.

A world unknown and ubiquitous to some, but known all along since the beginning—

The calling down of the dark shadows, for many times before, the phoenix has risen atop the pyramidal axis of the constructed sphinx. Great mysteries and power dwell there,

Entwined with the existence of faith in past soul warriors, time has woven its greatness in all who believe.

GREETING

Reintroduce yourself, please, to them—not you.
Are we not strangers to this place called world?
Within this being lies the stranger yet to unravel; among the unknown
dwells a child beneath.
We all inhale and exhale—not at the same time, but in this space—so
let not differences separate.
Provide a link where one can look to another's face and not think, who?
Are you? They are? But know it is.
Therefore, let us reintroduce ourselves to places that we share here in
the world.

THE UNIVERSE IS CONTROLLED BY GOD

He realigns all things to rectify what has been wronged.

If He were not a merciful God, He would eradicate those of greed of the flesh and man's lawless acts, but He is a forgiving God; those who are untrue too will quicken in His spirit and fall to their knees,

For what is written by him in the stars and universe is not determined by man and cannot be reversed.

Man cannot control fate or destiny.

The great God brings together spirits that have been already written; He unites and pieces those puzzles together to fit forever eternally, He fashions great souls in the likeness of Him.

Meticulously, He immerses the essence of light that His Holy Spirit transcends, and He anoints His flock; He has given prophesying powers to those who give of themselves completely.

Our father is so miraculous that at this very moment, He is controlling the words that pour onto this paper.

As I open the simplest of books, the miracles at hand are released through images and words from the Almighty Himself. I have witnessed through my spiritual eyes my Father's works at hand unfolding before me on this very day.

Once again, he has shown me my true love, destiny and future.

There are no coincidences—just me and my God, and when you believe in Him, He will set you free.

"One glimmer of light at a time," says He from above. "My dearest child, hold on. Everything is closer than you think. Do not wait on man, wait on me. What is true shall be as I promised you; all things shall come through me. The doors of eternal love are opened wide for you because you have faith in me. My child, you have filled me with complete and utter joy. I love you as I adore my son, for you too are my child, and I have set you free."

HERE WITH YOU

The Divine has numbered the days when I wept, and as I slept, He touched the mind's eye to ensure another message.

Each thought is documented in His mind, a collection of memories kept by Him as a reminder of faith, for diligent warriors of God are honored by His great light and fiery love.

Such power drives us into the dwelling place of the inner soul.

He is the companion that we need and more

He welcomes lepers and outcasts from lonely worlds.

As a reminder, He is there to show that He will always be there when man has written us off.

HOLD ON

For all that we can see is hidden deep in the chest; behind there lies immense torment.

The continuous search for a familiar soul is impossible.

Faces and forms in the sphere are as peculiar as religion, but miraculous are we that our spirits soar inward to soothe the pain.

A lover's heart is as deep, as sullen weights of a metal anchor, but the anchor leaves the pit in the soul with the name engraved inside.

Separate are the hearts in space and time, never meeting or agreeing.

Faith gives strength, while some want the mind, form, and being to fast-forward.

Past is the past, some say, but it makes up the character toward growth, where inner strength lies.

So when we are free, the smile gives way to peace within the soul, where no one but God Himself can understand the makings of the spirit.

Inseparably pure is the light, and when we find it, we do not let it go.

INTANGIBLE

Prickly pointed objects—that's what I am, unable and shielded from the human touch, not comprehensible, but ambiguous in some uncanny way.
But a yearning for a higher love is the craving—
Nothing forced, just naturally beautiful.
Left breathless,
Breaks in the skin emit light. The skin lets out the energy, like an exhalation from the lungs.
Before contact happens, it must contain truth without altered states; complex as we are, mankind is at its best when in simplest thoughts, like an innocent child who is intangible and untouched.
The pointed edges are being smoothed out to reflect the light from above, for this very notion is known to be absolute.

JANE

It was you who covered my open wounds.

The pain in your eyes, you endured for sure. Taking on the entire world, your shoulders could very well break.

Life's hardships and choices sometimes lead to mistakes. Nevertheless, observing silently yet cautiously, you read through souls.

Life's disappointments shaped you.

Mother, I have watched you hold in pain when you lost a true love. A life of happiness that once was has passed by—your very thoughts were, "No need to ask why."

Another chapter closed but still alive in your spirit.

Although tears did not fall, I cried for you through it all.

But peer closely—one can see your whole life in your eyes. You're a crown jewel, a queen in all of my sight, a visionary that is gifted by God; you are graciously breathtaking, full of insight.

Your tenacious abilities are marked by continuity as you uphold the family as best you can.

Why, there are so many hats you wear, no wonder God smiled when creating you. You're a chef, interior decorator, doctor, psychologist, and lawyer.

Of course mistakes are made, but each day you grow good, better, and best.

I must confess, you will forever be in my chest. To hold you high is what I do, I owe all of myself to one that's true.

Some may think you could have been more; I say you have lived life with no approval required.

Cumbersome individuals are no barricade for you; your quick wit throws the curve ball every time.

This is why you are remarkably sublime.

Raising girls into women was a job and challenge; without you, what would we do?

Sacrifice has taught you to teach me to wait patiently.

Amazing, that's what you are.

One can never know how you delve into pain silently; nevertheless, your strength and words reign inside endlessly.

My thoughts you know, my heart, soul, and mind—

Having this beacon of light that is your mind, you have passed down the torch.

I am overwhelmed by your resilience. You are every woman I want to be, and more.

Many may not comprehend this mystery: why everyone contemplates to unravel the puzzle. The answers lie in the DNA of my miraculous, beautiful, unforgettable, strong, influential, and powerful mother.

Radiance is exquisitely your name, Jane.

Your daughter,

Lisa

JOIN

Magnificent are Thee that cometh toward the light, for the fragrant rose is just a flower until it is plucked by a lover's hand,
Gentle like the petals, but the embrace is vehemently violent like the thorns.
Oh, how sweetly urged is the heart led into disarray, fallen down and weeping vulnerably, for neither you nor I are spoken for, but merely strangers of tomorrow, bewildered and lost, some might say.
Nevertheless, beyond somewhere far in time, another life waits to unfold a great palace without ambiguity—

LISTEN

Hear all things around you.

Be like the man who cannot see for the sounds of life are like music, from a child's cry to a sparrow gently settling on a tree branch.

Why indulge and use your ears? Imagine them as being eyes.

Learn to appreciate many strange voices and sounds, not just those you truly hear.

Listen to the sounds in your head—they are but imaginings and whispers of your cognitive thought patterns.

One can hear and listen to music in the mind where there is none, like Mozart.

Like the third eye, the ears share an extra sense that becomes sight for the insightful, so remember, the joyous sounds are visionary experiences through listening.

LIKE CHILDREN

Be like children. We should look to what is pure in spirit and filled with light, for these little beings work and play with the best.

In their minds, love always exists.

They frolic fancy-free by night and day.

The little ones are not troublesome, though at times they might tamper with mischief.

Nevertheless, they are completely and utterly fulfilled by the simplest aspects of life. We can learn from them.

Their minds are so open and sharp that they create beings that communicate within their own world.

The conscious and unconsciousness are dream states.

They embody all that is pure, for each day, they imagine and toil with the angels from above.

We all should adopt this behavior and emulate the little children.

LITTLE DID SHE KNOW

A woman speaks in terms of endearment for her life some time ago that has been lived.

She believes no one can ever replace her beloved. In the heart is where he will stay—her life and her love.

Do we ever ponder that we might meet another mate later in life?

The fabric of life is woven by Him who emits all things naturally.

God brings forth another life to those who believe in Him; He'll drive the forces of the heart where they will find themselves connected, for some think that after the golden years, such happenings are not feasible. Nonetheless, with God, all things are possible.

He opens the door for those to step through. With just a glance across the room at someone you knew all along He can ignite your spirits and will those souls as one.

One woman finds a love and realizes that God sent him for her before her spouse's twilight was coming to its end.

He from above arranged everything for her—little did she know that once again she was going to find a best friend.

Pleasingly, from heaven's window, her husband peers through to give his blessing for her to find love another day, for the golden years are not the time when one should give up on love

The deserved receive such blessings and no time is wrong for God

If it is on His time, then the time is always right

Love has found her once more—little did she know.

LOOK UP

Has the universe failed another?
Gentle souls reach up to fly, but drown in a never-ending point of no
return.
Choice, you say, what choice when the only feeling is pain?
Now, that is reality, where you know you existed in some time or space—
Uncanny and profoundly the joining of spirits hold like tight junctions
in the anatomy—intangible, but in the mind, love is believable.
Or is it?
As yesterday creeps into your sphere, try to hold on to that essence and
timeless tomorrow, for cherished experiences and truth are all you need
Oh, universe, you tell all that is in the soul for the eyes to see—im-
mersed in him completely.
Learn to look up and not down, for the cosmos has aligned its stars for
the pure in heart.

LOVE AND SCIENCE

You are in my veins, flowing through every vessel, capillary, and artery
Why, you are like science! How knowledgeable to my mind you are.
But it is the contracting of that very muscle within my cavity you hold
in your hands—
For when each beat pulsates, you're pumping life through my veins
Every thump of my heart is a force of respiration entering my lungs to
bring forth my breath,
If this is not science intertwined with love, then what is?
The never-ending circulation of you runs through all of my being as
though it were a rush of adrenaline. Now, is that not one of the amino
chains?
You are positive feedback, igniting and signaling the neurons that
transmit electrical pulses to my heart. The nerve endings are conduct-
ing the stimulation of thought to the mind.
Dendrites are sending further signals to all other sensations of the
body, for the brain has been encoded with the memory of your touch,
smell, and taste.
But during the dream state, when REM takes over, I hear you in my
thoughts and envision you in the mind; this is when auditory comes to
play.
You have taken over all my senses as you flow through me.
Like science, you speak a personal language within my anatomy; you're
controlling my form and leaving me in a state of homeostasis.
Why, you stabilize my central being every time.
For science and love are timeless. Both are entangled for all eternity,
winding together in the double helix of the DNA of man and woman.
This is why you are science to me.

You necessitate and complete all of my anatomy; while you continue to run through my veins pulsate in my heart, stimulate thought to mind, you bring forth breath to my lungs and from my lips, I whisper your name.

MARKED

The pit of this stomach is tied up in knots as if ready to go.
Unchanging, this being welcomes or chooses a fate unwisely.
It is evident that the stomach ousts and expels what is unnatural. All biological and systemic functions release foreign toxins.
This is how the marked one's intuition is heightened by the almighty; like that of the signaled synapses passing through neurons in the form; the blueprint and the process of cellular life has been planned for man's continuation.

> To a great extent, men are not the creators or map to one's existence; He that knows all has numbered the hair strands on our head, the design of a fingerprint, and compassion in a beating heart is His work.

Thus, it is intrinsically His plan for the universe and all that dwells within His light.
This leaves us to question if our destiny is hung atop of a tree while some doubt the power of the Most High?
Some have uttered statements of untruth to toil with the psyche and test the loyalty and faith given from above while strategies of coercion and persuasion fail.
Many look on licentiously with covetous eyes, losing our Father's favor and falling short of His grace. They mark us while marking themselves. For impurity and lewdness do not intermingle with a creature of God. One says to the stars, It is for you. If not from our father, the act lacks truth. For thou art blessed and protection is given by the Almighty One from falsehood
Many look at us as a mystery that will unfold before our eyes—

Cursed, you say, no, blessed, I say, do not mock the wonders of the Great One

BEHOLD, His glory is the mark of mystical treasures that await those who believe in His works at hand.

The interchanging of eyes cold like glaciers are nothing to his children. As passersby try to piece together this great puzzlement, it is but a waste of time.

Is it only derision that an unbeliever has to offer?

Only He can unlock all that is not comprehensible; His knowledge goes beyond all understanding.

A path from outside forces are false, the chosen course is foretold since birth.

The universe does not force the unnatural; such tactics are released superficially, like toxicity in the air depleting life.

For the universe is the Great One's creation; it pleases Him to witness His creatures working together harmoniously, not giving in to rash or intolerable behavior.

The mind of God is in our thoughts at all times, as if light illuminates words of secrecy that only He and His creatures share.

A burning desire is then ignited in the soul to draw all who love Him deeply to the spirit.

So there are none who control the universe but the One that is most efficacious in the creation of it.

For this reason, we gladly take any mark where many can witness His works—

The fortitude given by the Great One is taken in honor, for He is the bearer and key to our salvation.

METEOR

How intolerable are you?

For one is comparable to a meteor that has fallen from above; from the universe comes a fiery rock, plummeting down, burning through flesh to bone.

It is only the coolness of a kiss that soothes this unbearable heat.

In one's absence, the cycle begins again, for the falling rock symbolizes the heart.

Or like a falling angel, one rises up like a phoenix from the ashes.

All around the furnace lives this great pain.

Miraculously, the fallen rock begins to alter in appearance, slowly breaking into two, like cellular division. In these divisions, forming are great lights, becoming one where pain gives way to contentment,

For two have finally met, once again entwined in bliss.

MIND TRAVEL

To live in your cranial nerve is what I want. Traveling in your mind is where I'll unlock your mystery.

I am like the pulsating electricity of that neuron that signals your dendrites—

Axon and I are linked as one.

This is how I want to know your every thought.

My behavior is now revealed, for I possess your mind's whims, feelings, and wit.

Not controlling, that's not it, but being and living in every moment that excites you, makes you happy, makes you smile or feel your vulnerability—

Why, one experiences all of your being and sensations throughout your existence.

I am the nerve endings igniting all over you in motility, angst, and pleasure.

How delightful to be in you and know the bitter and sweetest of moments—

When you pain, I pain, your aches, my aches, your love, my love.

For this mind travel is the only way to be near and in you, utterly and inexplicably, my love.

MISGUIDED BY REASONABLE DOUBT

Has the unseen guided those who are blind? Or is it the closed mind and heart that cannot see?

Joy fills the breasts of those who are from the brokenhearted. The pain fades like the fog and mist burning out in the sun's rays.

Away with the old self an innate hidden treasure will manifest for the world to see—

It is a shedding of skin to birth one in transformation.

Only the Great One knows the path to the natural destination.

One can feel the calling deep down in earth's core, the center where the light holds infinitely.

Miracles are no coincidences, but they are proof of true faith and love for the spirit, so see—peer closely where guides and signs are all about, beyond reasoning, leaving no room for doubt.

MOMENT

Give rest in Him when you grow lonely and weary, let out your troubles in the world and focus your mind for a moment.

Soar as a bird does, through the ocean in the soul.

Go catch it! Oh, what exhilaration to feel the life of love streaming through the veins.

Infinitely, those in the know are looking up to the sky, so forget your troubles, fears, and bothersome thoughts of the world.

Live through the voice of those who have followed Him long ago.

The secrets of the moments are experienced and shared through you and Him.

MORE

There is more inside—many sides that are conflicting with reality. this form lives partiality;

Life lessons come with responsibility; choices and decisions are linked with ambiguity.

Where does it begin? Where should it end?

Should one be considered as a package? Like a gift wrapped up, outside pretty, but inside filled with uncertainty?

Sensuality and light are entwined in the center of this package. Inside lies the darkness reaching toward the light of truth.

One's soul is but a dismal existence longing for the whispers. Challenges are sweet and bitter victories resolved from triumphant war.

A package unopened is a mystery untold and ready to unfold, but it takes one to unravel the package gently without disturbance of the inner light, for aggression is but a animalistic quality that is of no other than desperate measure.

Nurture suffices and gives way to pleasure once the package is held sincerely.

What is this package made from, with its satiny bows on its top? Why, one wonders, what is in the package?

Stories told, reputations hold, but does the tongue utter the truth?

Oh my, what a package—the human soul comparable to a cardboard box?

It is neither flesh nor bone and does not contain the beating heart as its core center. Why, the center holds the soul's light, waiting to burst through splendidly.

It is not wise to consider a person package, it is merely an object. we are all made to be special and not comparable to a package that is topped delicately with an appealing bow.

So before you consider opening the package, think carefully and be sure, for once it is ajar, the light will captivate you and draw you in for more.

MURDERERS OF PASSION: A TRIBUTE TO THE ARTISTS

A true artist celebrates life each day.

A stranger's face, landscapes, nature, everything represents beauty. Before his very eyes life, experiences become his palette. Images depict both surreal and realistic mediums.

But it is not until the passion-mongers eradicate every creation of the artist, then life has no meaning for his existence.

They rob them with these policies of how life is to be lived, for normalcy is forced on them and forsakes their gifts that are given from above. Society dictates conformity, and with it comes stagnation, angst, and a suffocation of creativity.

The soul becomes suppressed when it cannot express—it is the passion of talent gone to waste and murdered.

The system envies the ones who are blessed with God's gifts and frowns on those creatures. Economists find them not worthy in contributing to society—they are neither bankers nor physicians who would save lives.

What importance are they?

Sadly, mistaken by those who are not from the world of artists, such assumptions are false, for artists make for a delightful existence. They have yet to comprehend the soul of the artists.

Why try to dissect and observe such beings like projects? Their significance is simply that they bring joy, enrichment, and beauty to life, for they embody and replicate the true artist who paints the sky with His Almighty hand.

Made by him are the creations of delicate fragrant flowers with the colors of rainbows, and the varied insects that pollinate them.

The replication of Himself is placed in the spirits of all who are skilled.

The artists are God's students and were chosen from their mothers' wombs.

They emulate His works that make magic through them: on a painted canvas, with music on an instrument or a voice like an angel, or in the sculpted human form, or through words by a composer or from an author's book.

An artist struggles to find himself through his art, for he and the art are one.

Artists display love, pain, joy, sorrow, and pleasure in all forms of art. Conformity is not of their nature unless beckoned for survival.

We who are artists are banded together to raise our voices as one. A safe haven is found among us, where we are drawn near like skin to bone.

The murderers of passion suck us dry until the very life force is no more. We will resist them to the end.

In an artists' world they create, the rush of life returns like air inflating the lungs to breathe once more.

Artists' will express in all forms of art where we embody the power of what God truly placed in each and every one of our souls whence we came to be the ARTISTS:

Why stamp out passion?, watch out! We the artists will take a stance and repel conformists.

MYSTERIOUS BIRD

A bird flies; it's no ordinary bird. This creature hears and feels the vibrations of the earth

It sees and is the eye of mankind; he peers down from the skies, keeping watch for the brokenhearted.

This gentle feathery creature is different—he is sent by God.

Remarkably, he dashes swiftly in a flash, fine-tuning his built-in navigation to hone in on the so-called undesirables. With it, his electromagnetic messages are sent up above

He communicates the thoughts of the unwanted by society to the Divine One, and in this process, he makes a line of connection to the spirit realm.

Oracle creature obeys instantaneously, for the creature's sole purpose is to give hope to the unloved and unfortunates here on earth.

As he reports to our Father in the great skies that there is dire need for the fallen ones, our Father swoops in with mighty hands to embrace all, filling the void of those with lonely hearts.

NIGHTINGALE

Oh, gentle nightingale, why is it that you amaze me?
Just before dawn you remind me of all that is beautiful. As I open my
eyes, your music captivates me, and my soul is touched by your gentle
song.
As I lie down, you're a reminder that I am not alone.
Your song rings in my spirit, a lost memory of true love.
Thoughts are extracted from my mind and translated into emotions.
Never leave oh gentle nightingale. I look for your song to bring forth
life to one who has lost faith in love.

NOTHING LEFT BUT THE SOUL

Idle and still unknown to existence, were Adam and Eve created for the mere purpose of a union?

Those who are controlled nevertheless will not comprehend, but ah, it is within the beats of the heart. That expression is no mystery.

The mind of the Master one should not question, but only those who are silent are known to be deep like the waters. These waters can be murky and dark.

It is this very day that ponders continuously like the second-hand on a clock, ticking away.

Why is it that the forefathers and foremothers before us lay down to bring forth great generations? What was it for?

Are we united? Did we not get it? Are we just empty vessels of energy wasted throughout space?

The purity of the heart should be the inspiration, as our true Father cleaves us from within his very being.

Matters around all of the earth in space would have not gone to waste. When all is said and done, nothing is left but the soul.

OBJECTS

Objects are nothing until the hand brings them alive. They are created by man, but useless without the interaction.

Similarly, the sun is pointless without light, for the dark cannot bring life like the glorious light of the great star.

Objects can be many things, some toil with them to help or make their lives better.

Truth and the nature of things do not hide but step out from behind the self, but when man's wants and desires are obsessive, the innocence no longer exists.

A person too can be like an object; in this case, the importance of love is not profound.

Better to have faith than to yearn for inanimate things or to hope for possessed objects you can never obtain.

Possession of the form is not from the light, so kneel and pray that the spirit is opened wide not to crave the worldly preoccupation.

Persistence does not contain patience or perseverance.

Opposite of such actions is to build a character as strong as iron, for ostentatious display of force produces negative discourse actions reverse the psychological mind-set and open the door to truth by staring in the mirror.

Give charity it's just due and let life unfold on its own. Sacrifice life's truest lesson, where words can satisfy intimacy, and do not look for false acts.

Search for the true light from above, where calculating does not exist.

OBSERVER

A detail of your expertise is recorded and ingrained in the mind. With just a stroke, a paintbrush forms images so authentic one is locked in. Miraculously, the magic within his delicate hands are God's creation. Cleverly the skilled one makes life pour onto the canvas—streams of colors in the sky, and water realistic as though one could step in to feel the coolness of its temperature, the blues of its sky and sun so bright one has to shield the face.

How the observer marveled, watching the skilled one's hands make miracles and images come to life.

Can one say the beautiful one is a prodigy? Or is it just instinctual that God creates one to emulate nature and life with such skill?

Needless to say, the observer is left to gasp in awe every time.

OMNIPOTENT ALLURE

In the presence of darkness, your radiance imposes a ray where the purest of souls are set free. Drawn in by this light, unification takes place; like honey stirred in milk, how sweetly urged is its taste.

Together you and I can conquer all the matters within paradise—
Exquisitely, we possess what is rare, like jewels found in lost treasures, unknown like a mystery, but solved by our history.

One gaze into your eyes and I explode with the intensity like that of the Big Bang or spontaneous combustion. Your spirit is so bright that it lights up all of the Milky Way, drawing me to your path.

You personify an essence that is alluring to all. The Great One planned wonders for these delicate creatures.

Omnipotent is the nature of this union; what else could there be?

ORCHESTRA CONDUCTED

There's a long line of magnificent composers just beyond the clouds in heaven. The spirited masters are performing for the Master of masters. In the heavens you'll find great music unheard of and never played on earth, for the Divine One's home is of royalty.

The greats and not-so-greats display their gratitude to him; expressed is their joy to receive such gifts of music where one could find or hear strings, percussion, and pianos,

Not to mention a few other instruments, such as the horns of triumphs, played exquisitely by chosen musicians.

Gleefully, the Divine One looks on with pride and amazement that He touched their souls creatively to express musical ingenuity.

So happy is He that when He laughs, a great thunder comes from the clouds. That is how much joy the Divine One feels.

The sounds in heaven are but sweet angels, choosing the instruments they love and playing them so effortlessly for their King.

PARADOX

A blissful and sublime creation from the spirit—
How pure is this word "Love," as beautiful as the holy light from above.
The soul pours out the glow and generates radiance around all. The paradox of the mind's thoughts is questionable when acted on.
Troublesome words can create ambiguity within their content. Are they false or true?
Like scientists or philosophers, they are searching for factual proof,
Enabled or handicapped to walk through the doorway, barriers broken down.
Even those who are disabled are able in the mind.
The mind's third eye creates a paradise of enchantment that emits peace and captivates the soul to inspire peace.
Paradox is a matter of fact that can realistically work in many ways in life.

FATHER: PERSONAL KNIGHT

July 23, 2008—This very day is marked as monumental, and this is when heaven's doors opened and from it came my father, **James Lee Alexander**, my personal knight, guardian, warrior, and hero.

Gosh, words cannot explain how much I adore you, for God gave you a will that is made of steel and a heart of melting snow. You are from all things that are naturally beautiful in this world.

When life has been a rock and a hard place, your gentlest words soothed its blow.

You are king to me, looking down to make sure that I am guarded, for the Most High sends your very voice to my mind as a premonition.

When in danger, it is your words that I hear; they protect me. Your guardianship is so precious that all the money in the world cannot be enough, for you are priceless. You exude every quality that is good. Your heart and emotions flow through like molten rock of a volcano. This is how powerful you are.

You are my personal warrior and hero, who is fearless and true to your words. God has knighted you the protector of all.

For all people love you, young and old. They see the great one reigning inside your very being, your soul.

Your spirit draws all things that are pure to you. This is why as you walk this earth, the little angels follow and cherish you.

Remember, you have been knighted by the King of kings from the Most High, for you are knighted as a king for the children's heart by the Almighty.

Father, I love you and truly adore you for all eternity.

Happy Birthday

Your daughter,

Lisa Alexander

PLUCKED

In a time when nothing is left, "Look to me," says a voice from above.
Below, there's turmoil where one should flee. In there, the days are long
as if it were years of endless turmoil, though if the Great One's flock
should mistakenly travel to Hades, the fiery place will have to give in
to the wrath, trembling in fear when our Heavenly Father retrieves his
child.

He will vouch for an innocent spirit every time.

The furnace awakens a greater self, evolving into a higher state of being.
Then one is plucked from the bowels of the cursed one and released—
The soul is then lifted and drawn to the home of the Excellent One.

PUPIL

Teach me. I am your pupil. All the knowledge you contain, I want to know. Everything you feel within your heart I too want to feel.

I want to go through your heart like the pulse of its beats.

Your mind is but a mystery, and no one knows—only you. This too I need to know—

Whatever food you indulge, let me be that food that enters your lips, so with that food I could sample the sweetest taste you experience in life through them

Ah, but your eyes are most important, for the pupil gets to witness what they see

They display love to all things near and touched by you

I want to be your ears so that I could hear all sounds of nature, music, or whatever brings you joy and make you smile

My love, your nose is most important—with it, your senses are aroused, and your spirit is released when you smell the gentlest aromas of God's creation, the rose,

What could be sweeter for a pupil than to experience the aroma of love?

This too would be the ultimate lesson for the pupil, for any pupil would be eager to learn all things from you.

QUENCH

The heart is pleased when you're in my presence.

In you and around you dwells the holy one, for the heart satisfies those of likeness, and no other milk will do; a babe only enjoys his mother's drink.

Familiar ones crave or thirst for what is known in the spirit, not the stranger,

Glorified is this great heart where this splendid love lasts forever and many days lingering; still awaiting for the ultimate quenching—

At last, one says, you have come to saturate me with your inner glow; oh how foolish you have made this being alive in the chest! Can one only know the power you contain in your words and light?

Manifestations of an angelic soul pour out silken syllables unknown to mankind until one staggers in a drunken state, like that of one who has danced around a bottle of the wicked brew too many times.

Is it a bewitching state or an effect of toxicology that brings about ambiguity in the head? A befogging, as you may, where the will is ousted forever.

By God, whatever it is in this brew; one can never lose its taste or urge for more. It is a bittersweet deliciousness never tasted until one has encountered your kiss.

Truly the thirst is no longer but has been quenched by this delicate creature in long pasts due.

QUESTION

Occurrences—are they apart of reality's landscape or the spirit world?
Is it fate that those incidents come to play?
What is surreal or real? Like Salvador Dali's paintings we can perceive our own opinion, so what are these occurrences? Are they objects or numbers speaking in a silent voice loudly for one to see?
Is it coercion speaking with an ill-repulsed voice?
Can one determine through objects that there are, in fact, signs? Reminders are all around—unknown to the viewer—or are they to torture one's soul? Does one acknowledge a familiar name in a reception area, the number on a vehicle, the brand name of water from the past? This is why everything must be questioned.
Why such mockery? It is but a joke, and what a waste of one's time. Unfortunately, it is the ghastly part of human nature, not appealing in the least. Only time will tell when the surreal merges with the real—and only one can stand alone.
He above will bring forth the geniuses of the situation at hand, and such beings will be exposed for all to view, for God knows the ways of man; He will be there at every corner they turn.
There are those to whom loyalty means the world and others to whom it means nothing. Many will do anything to have such bliss falsely. Why live superficially?
Sadly, that would be to search for something that is imagined within the mind. Then such sentiments are pretentious and are not from the pure soul.
But to contain foul and empty emotion is nothing but revolting; the universe does not warrant imitation acts, for it is He that fashioned the universe with His hands with care, and it is created naturally through love.

It is He that controls His creatures' comings and goings. Toiling and tinkering with the mind and heart—that is not a part of His plan.

Opponents are aware of such happenings and chuckle when we suffer. Bewildered and speechless, the opponents are left asking and searching for the truth.

The oracle is truth, and testimony is strength of the spirit that He carved from His very chest to place in my own.

With anticipation the viewer angst emerges out of control—

Do they not know that the Father is the rock?

Such behavior goes unrecognized beneath cunning nature.

Enemies are those who cannot think of the purity of spirit and dwell beneath the vile uncleanness scouring the earth for flesh. Why waste such energy on things that are deceitful and of shallow emotions?

Some feel connected because of one's self and want to claim ownership, but it is the core of the heart, where the character dwells, that is untainted.

When it is free, the power of true love has wings, for this very notion, money cannot buy the human heart or comprehend what is in the soul. One has to question such happenings within their natural state.

Nevertheless, in the spirit state, and in God's world, they watch over the beings that dwell beneath the heavens.

Many may know your mind and heart, so they toil endlessly to confuse reality, for they know that the mind and will are strong, because God is the solidifier.

Then those occurrences from above are just a test of loyalty of the spirit and character that will stand as strong as the pillars in heaven.

QUILT

Dedication with complications, obstacles, and pinnacles, scholar approved by society's honor—
Empowerment and alignment, the stars fall and rise like the great sun. Oh how magnificent in the mind if the world would embrace all that is uncanny.
There will come a day when some may behold His grace for many; in the meantime, the wheels turn as controversy brings about calamity until Luther's dream is really true.
Unravel like sands or graves under our feet; are we not all the same?
What is in the matter of separatism? Even the jealous skies make way for the hungry sun. It burns in the soul's eye, a resplendent passion.
Look out and see the lands where many write, paint, sculpt, and capture the essence of beauty. Beyond it, there are many mysteries untold within.
Let's join in like those from a rainbow, for all are children derived from its grandeur.
Past, present, and future is learned for the scholars, but one cannot understand the meaning of life through actual books and experimentation. As many say, life is to be lived gloriously, for this great quilt and fabric we all share on this earth together.

REACH THROUGH THE RIVER

Life comes with bitterness and pleasures waiting to unfold.

Grief stricken in utter torment; the wound that causes pain opens up the human consciousness, for pain and misery later begins to wither away like melting snow come spring; giving way to rain.

Drops falling in the river give rise to the unknown.

In anguish, the sweeter taste of life is just beyond reach, getting closer. Mystery produces a pleasing scent and a flavor that gently falls on the tip of one's tongue like honey.

Familiarity relieves one where complacency takes place within the self.

Angst and pierced in the heart; a bridge is extended to form foundations. Miraculous transformations commence where the ultimate lesson is to realize that one's heart is just as human and vulnerable as the next.

For the river symbolizes life's indeterminacy: an interweaving and evolving of temporary phases, but leading toward the spirited path, completing its journey in the character building.

A reaching for a lit passage; contending within one self; a breakthrough to rediscover anew—

REASON

From the time of the beginning, the act of it all is to follow his way.
What other reason could there be?
Sublimity unfolds, man's beauty, strength, and zest for life is His plan.
What drives you is the human spirit and soul of him living within.
Stop searching and dive in the pool of wonders, says he. I'll be your
doctor of doctors, teacher of teachers, and love of all lovers.
For I am all that you should draw near to; think not of the world, but
only put your all in me.
I determine one's fate, and I am the maker of everyone's mind.
I am your truest desire and destiny, and heaven is home within your
beating heart, the reason for it all, everything above and below.

REASSURANCE

Your voice is but music to my ears. The sound has a song that is unforgettable.

Yearning for that familiar melody, the spirit is soothed into a gentle trance.

Surrendering to your will burns an inner light that consumes all of the soul. Who can deny such a passion for everlasting love?

It is so welcoming that its fortress is a place that I can always call home.

Inevitably, this is always a space that I long to cling to; the feeling is of warmth from a gentle touch by an angel who hears silent cries and answers prayers.

Vividly the mind pictures the makings of the little miracles, but it is only the remembrance of your voice, Father that leaves one rendered and consoled.

For the time we are here; we must wait and listen. We may be among the living for a time; however, waiting and listening for your voice is what all should look for to help when facing adversity.

RECYCLED

(Create something out of "Spinning Senselessly")

In time, in space, like matter, allowing for no apparent direction, winding, twisting, and turning in a motion of complexity—
Fragmented elements tossed back and forth in frenzy, similar to a tornado wreaking havoc on a tranquil village, this great spinning breaks the peace like shrieking noise and screeching metal.
Is it the force of nature that is at hand or is it artificial intelligence?
Destination nowhere and out of control amid the unknown, but familiar objects are taken under with water consuming all things in its space—
Spherically forming and rising within the aqueous environment, the shapes merge.
Why, they create an iridescent image, and in it they reflect various objects, for these mysteries are unexplainable and unpredictable.
The tumultuous power of motion beckons for peace; however, still lost until a sudden stillness and calmness takes over, and then once again the counteractions cease chaos, and order makes sense once more until the final spin.

Author of "Spinning Senselessly": Claude Saccaro
Poem by: Lisa Alexander

RELIGION AS A VEIL

Some say we conceal ourselves behind religion. I say religion is a safe haven for our souls to be consumed immensely.

Many times, one may find solace within the doctrines of the word from above; as one evolves, the Holy Spirit delivers emergence on a spiritual realm.

No one can explicate the powers of the unseen spirit that surrounds us in God's presence.

The veil is not a mask, but a protection to buffer the negative forces that try to penetrate the world of God's children.

Purposefully, there are those who judge what they know not of; they only see through the eyes of the judgers.

Walk in the footsteps of your brother and see the impact of life and torment filled with pain, for only he knows that through anguish we are awakened blissfully in our Master's presence.

But the veil serves as an angel's wing, concealing and protecting us from the darkness

Religion encompasses all that people cannot offer-the spirit is strong on a level that no one can imagine

To share in the world of a child of God, it is not through the flesh. One must enter from the spirit; then you may truly understand the works from Him because you are a part of Him.

The powers that tend to mix reality with fantasy are to only justify their cause. We are ones who have little power and witness the controls within society, but it is He who acts on our behalf to set things right. One has to develop one's own world to escape the world designed for the breaking point.

The veil then becomes a force field to block out unwarranted beings, for religion is the ultimate veil that protects the body, the mind, and the Holy Spirit that dwells within each and every child of God.

REPEL

Those very things that we run from should we walk toward? Is it the nomadic nature to continue to escape one's true self?

Search to find Him. He dwells in the breast and in the mind's eye, for contentment embarks wonders that are untold

Why it is that man believes that they are the true interpreters?

Destiny has been aligned with the universe, it is known within man's soul—the beginnings of sudden transformations entwined with the inner light. Pathways are submersed with the knowledge of wisdom and are burned in the very thought of man.

Are we really saved? Or is man's notion of dedication just an act of formality? Can we then capture the essence of divinity within the burning desire in the heart?

Continue to look upward to the stars; they do not defy. Unlike man, they are unchanging.

For Him, the powers are ingrained and burned in the fibers of the mind.

Touch not what is tainted; leave clean and pure in the light of the Great One, care for each other and repel things of this world—

Preeminently, the word truth holds up and repels all materialistic longings.

ROOTS AND GROUND

Now I am exposed; it is only your eyes that penetrate my inner being.
No other could comprehend how we can peel away at the soul, take the
heart from the thoracic cavity, and toss it away like rubbish.

Fallen to the earth, an unfolding of the heart occurs: the left and right
atriums attach to the ground to fertilize roots of love, arteries and veins
are pumping the life liquid into the earth to form new souls for the
brokenhearted.

A gushing sound splatters around looking for empty vessels to grab
hold of—

These beings are not ordinary hosts; they are reborn from hearts' tormented states, but these new forms embody a fiery soul of the phoenix
rising—

Joining together by vessels and arteries, all are evolving into a glow that
light up the dark spirit.

RUNNING FROM YOUR INNER BEING

Somehow we all seem to be running onto an endless bridge.
We should concern ourselves with enlightenment.
Time is of the essence and not to be squandered on such thoughtless gestures
How is it that the path intertwines back to where it began?
Unmistaken but chosen by One who weaves the great fabric of life,
The creatures small and tall toil within their universe. He sometimes watches with a frown; nevertheless, some of those He created have brought Him joy
You who are lost and running from your inner being do not look beside, or down to the ground look up to the one who guides your steps
Hand selected and the very few are from the stock - a mold of unique antiquity
For there are those who have been crafted meticulously in his likeness
He marveled at that very day and was amazed with his creations
In his delight and filled with glee, unbeknownst to even the great one himself the bridge that returns is only the light that guides one home to him
Praise is what draws one to the bridge it evokes the true soul, therefore the bridge one runs is not endless, however it is timeless
Once crossed it restores the inner being each time
For the many that run from the inner being it is not genuine in the least
But when you have crossed the bridge to enlightenment that is the one place where the inner being will find lasting joy

SAVE MYSELF FROM MYSELF

Grievance awakens humility; suffering is a birthright that dives into the stream of iniquity. Without the turbulent wave of obstacles, the quest of life dulls the thirst.

Subjugations are the true essence of confirmation for the chosen path. It necessitates the quality of despair where there is spiritual growth emerging.

The soul sparks with a calling that whispers to the inner spirit, and in the calling, the spark is ignited into a fiery torch from God.

For saving the self is found in selfless deeds to humanity. All consciousness writes its way in the mind and opens a doorway to enlightenment. Like children who are in the world of the knowing, they find themselves every time, for they are saved from the time they exit their mothers' wombs untouched and pure, touched by a stronger being that is known to contain unseen powers unfolding.

In belief, the sufferings and grievance are unknown to those saved, but for the few, come back to the early days when life was new—search no more, for the light is dwelling within you.

SCARED STRAIGHT, THEY SAY

It is not for man to fear man, but to fear all who is in the knowing of man.

To chastise us and state the purpose uttered by man is not God's way. From the day he gives one first breath, sight, and hearing, He also placed in them intuitions.

The plan was mapped out for you by your spirit, placed within your mother who bore you. Not only does she alone adore you; even she knows not of the mysteries that lie ahead.

Oh, mockery brings about miracles, so to scare straight may be the plan of man, but it is He that makes the way, for paths are straight when one is true, for darkness will always give way to light.

Fear not man, only fear the One who creates the great works, for scared straight has brought out another you.

Many may marvel in disbelief when faith does not fold. It stands the test of time like the everlasting stars in the universe.

Like that of the great star, He resides in us the infinite light, so He has never left us in the great light, inside the sun, where the master plan of man's schemes cannot begin to understand.

Remember this: it is His molding a better you; the Great one aligns the universe to humble the most.

SCATTERED SEED

Every time we parted, my heart was shattered into a million pieces. The pain I could no longer withstand; fascinated by your very presence I am drowning in your glow.

Capture me in your net again—like a fish, as your bait but devoured by your soul—

Consume all of me. I want to be your prey, for my sorrow of you is but my joy. You bring me peace in a time of chaos.

Flood me with all of yourself like the floods from the risen sea where Noah built his ark. Drown me in your spirit once more; it is an honor to be in your presence and light forever, for you have placed in the soul the scattered seed where the heart has taken its root.

In it, the heart lingers and yearns for your existence, for you are the soil, and your spirit pours unto the seed like water quenching the thirst. You flow freely through, in, and around the seed, making it grow rapidly.

Its planting brings forth life when it ignites. This is when your light pours in.

Suddenly, the seed becomes a harvest of love. The seed has sprouted with the help of the great star to bring one closer, growing toward God's face.

SHELL

Work that mystical guidance over this life force, uncanny and strikingly omnipotent; fiercely you urged the words to flow like pouring water as natural as the glistening light of the stars.

The mind fires up like a connection of electrons as its outer shell. The activity and its concreteness unbreakable; leaves no room for vigilant ones.

Join in the whirlwind of the stirring of likeness to the three levels of the highest peak.

Interests are but witness to the Excellent One.

Sharpen the sharper; love eminently and steadfastly. All else will follow.

Anger toward nothing, strive toward nothing. Love all that is like the rainbow.

Look in the children faces; they are the answer if not tainted; in them He lives.

Leave in the heart the purity of the babe and the suckling.

Return, his voice says, return to grace and kneel down to honor him, crowning one with favor and glory to His kingdom; is His dominion over all.

SIMPLE

Lust for comfort till the day we are no more, search for work among strangers bearing no resemblance to him.

Are these vessels empty, to be filled with meaningless objects?

The wants and needs take precedence over the simplest things in life—Where the simple holds the pure soul; like a newborn child the simple just loves love.

The creature that lusts for comforts continues its fill but is never really full.

They crave cold objects that have neither soul nor spirit, for many work long and grueling hours to acquire these so-called pleasures.

Why suffer in this state of being?

How dismal and unnatural! Objects can't breathe, feel, smile, laugh, or cry. They just take up space and can never fill the heart.

Objects are just a reminder of suppression of human connection.

This is when the lust for comforts gives way to what is real—the simple pleasures in life.

SOLIDIFY

Build on something new until the floor crumbles from under your feet.
Is there any safe haven in this world of turmoil?
Be it known that the foundations only stand the test of time where
there is truth, for a word from Him can build mountains with oceans
that brush against the earth.
So as the earth is touched by the flesh from Thy feet, the earth too
crumbles and loses its base.
These are the forces of nature, and in life it is inevitable, for the circle
of life is to bring forth solidification and balance to all things.

SOUL GROWTH

As one walks down the spirited path, the soul grows, for each day is marked by a monumental moment to be one in His presence.

Fleeing emotions, like wings, are everywhere, touching those who come near and far.

Feelings of joy, sorrow, and compassion are but experience from deep down; the emotions that take flight are waiting to be captured by the glow that swims in the stream of love.

Purposely the directions are guided toward the everlasting wisdom and enlightenment, a fulfillment of promises left unbroken and delivered.

Life enchantment and rapture is encompassing growth within each moment, for one's fate could be as tumultuous as a storm and calming as silent raindrops.

But rest assured that the soul that hungers will leave no other remnants than pure authentic growth.

SPOILED BY SOCIETY

Physicians call it maladaptive behavior when they cannot understand.
Is everyone woven together like fabric? Misunderstood, some might
think; some call it interrupted, making one suffer and pay for misdeeds,
for the mind is but a jigsaw puzzle and is given a pill as an antidote.
Society embraces nothing of angelic nature, it only spoils and destroys.
One must travel the same road in life and be sure not to stray, for
uniqueness is rarely accepted.
Many a time, girl, boy, man, and woman are interrupted and experi-
mented on, unknown to us. Ah! But he is all knowing, for the eye is not
the man but it's the Father.
He is all knowing and is above, watching while you toy with the innocent ones.
Is all this for money when it can be replaced a hundred times over?
Humans are now subjected to serving as lab mice? Or is it a game of
chess but with lives?
Like monsters, seek out the innocent and conspire with those of darkness and not the light. Make them beg and plead on their knees for
forgiveness.
Leave one to be among wolves like sheep for predators.
Surely, there are matters much more pressing than the ones you find
amusing. Mind games are for the immature, unwise, and shallow-na-
tured individuals.
Many say they are knowledgeable and educated. I say most are not, for
a piece of paper does not define the truest character. Such individuals
are ignorant and like the tyrants from history past. They lack humility
and love in their heart toward mankind.
Oh while many stand by and play the game of capitalism to prove their
point, they just spoil and ruin lives as a means of vengeance. Their

mere existence has to be questioned and analyzed—heartless and sorrowful are their only existence.

Shamefully, they must not know love but only dream of it and never taste.

It's a pity for them to know what comes from above and is placed in a man's chest that is genuine. Once again one is spoiled by society in the name of reasoning.

STRIPPED

Without armor, under attack, and left vulnerable, in your presence one is just putty.

We can never withhold all of ourselves from you, no concealed secrets or treasures that you know not of, for hide and seek is just child's play.

But wait! One becomes the child and you, the controller of the game.

The armor begins to disintegrate for all to see, stripped away piece by piece, unveiling its ugly face before the world.

In nakedness, it is the truth that is stripped like a shark's teeth tearing through the flesh of man.

Slowly, yet gradually, the armor that was broken down is rebuilt! Again it is pieced together like a jigsaw puzzle; in a fragmented state, its luster is renewed.

The armor that was dismantled has been built once more by your mighty hand and better than before. It has been polished brightly where its blinding light leaves no man to see, but only for those who believe.

And you say, "Why wear this armor? You needn't protection any longer; your faith in me is all that you need, my child.

"Rest assured you can count on me. Your soul is your armor, for it is pure, so place your armor on the wall for others to see, for the faith that dwells inside is the true armor that the ones who don't believe can't see.

"This is your shield, and the fierceness of your beating heart is sacred. It is all the force that made this universe, and with this force is my eternal love from me to you."

TAKE THE HOURS

Take the hours, for none are returned; once spent, they are paid in full like a debt, my love, so spend them well. Slow down your rash eagerness and hasten not.

In the matters of the heart, trust that all is true and waste not, for precious time is to be consumed wisely on the tenderness, gestures, and moments.

Needless to say, yesterday reveal no precedence for the time being, which is the present.

Significantly, new times of excellence are lingering and waiting to be born again.

Be true within the hours. The brighter times are ahead, so take the hours and soar like an eagle, for you know the power of time and purpose.

For when the day comes—when twilights are closing—one's last breath is to take the hours that have been spent well and true.

THE LIGHT OF GOD

Search within yourself and find that you are truly free.

All strongholds loosen and shake at the very sound of God's rumbling thunder—so powerful that the seas part and many hide in fear of his wrath.

He's angry at those who delve into material and worldly affairs.

Release your souls to Him, for when the flock goes adrift, only He delivers you in a time of need. You are that perfect fabric that's interwoven in your mother's womb.

Amicably he lays you on your mother's breast as your second feeding, for your first feeding was his whispering your name to open your eyes. Those gentle words filled and gave birth to your spirit.

Gently He extracted you from the very sky that He created, for all things are from him, nature and spirit.

No holds are here on this earth.

Alone one is born until that day when the earth opens to swallow the form. Then the light of God will reach and take hold of your spirit and merge it with His own.

This is when you return home to him for all eternity in heavenly bliss.

RIVER OF LIFE

Life comes with bitterness and pleasures waiting to unfold.
Grief stricken, in utter torment, the wound that causes pain opens up the human consciousness, for pain and misery later begin to wither away like melting snow come spring.
In anguish, the sweeter taste of life is just beyond reach.
Mystery produces a pleasing scent and a flavor that gently falls on the tip of the tongue.
Familiarity relieves you where complacency takes place within the self
Angst, pierced in the heart, a bridge is extended to form foundations.
Miraculous transformations commence where the ultimate lesson is to realize that each heart is just as human and vulnerable as the next.
For the river symbolizes life, evolving on its spirited path to complete its journey.
Reach for a lit passage; contend with yourself—a breakthrough to re-discover anew.

THE UNFAMILIAR

Deep down in the depths of the earth lives the dark, lifeless soul long-ing for your presence and guidance.

A voice comes: dwell not with the earthly creatures, for they will devour your flesh and drain your spirit, soaking up all illumination, leaving a residue of murky encroaching emptiness—

A consumption of the forms is senseless when love is not an equation in the matter.

For purposeful, unfamiliar acts leave a void in the spirit.

Do away with peculiar appetites of the world, kneel down, and raise your head to the sky, for greatness is around those who seek the truth, as the Word gives life to all.

TO KNOW

Society is translucent around those who peer in to witness your existence.

For what reason are we here? Is there a purpose to find the winding road of hope?

Among many who are around, we are just strangers to the wind but not to the dust; while past life dictates the future—how else would we know life.

Each moment lived is embedded and encoded within at the cellular level. It is like the expectancy of childbirth; a woman never knows the outcome; nevertheless, she feels the life growing inside. Each birth differs from the next, and the same applies to the soul and the character.

No one is meaningless in their dwelling place when it comes to the Almighty God; He is highly exalted and directs us by subtle whispers in the spirit.

Psychologists, sociologists maybe perplexed about the human mind and thought pattern; however, only He that knows all creates the vessels.

Man is to see him as the benefactor in all rationality.

When one feels too immensely, the spirit becomes trodden like a walk on the soil or earth. Walls are closing; the world wants to create a black hole for many to fall through, but He disseminates the black hole and walls—

He places everything in its correct order to give meaning during disparity. In its center is where the light immerses and explodes everlasting energy and love.

TOIL

My love, you toil day and night, toiling with those of forced dwellings.
Your spirit is wasted on those not of your likeness.
Face thyself and be of valor. There'll be the days when neither sea nor earth shall part the soul.
It has been written and foretold before one ever knew. Complex as it seems, it has to be, and time grows near in the universe.
One cannot be sold or bought or owned—
The heart contains what the Creator has placed in its center.
Heed not the passages of the days, for Mother Earth nurtures and waits.
Another time, one of another season, may you find rest in this season in rapture—
For sabotage camouflage, the truth of the matter creeps forward and outward.
Toil no more, for life rewinds and circles to restore.

TOUCH THE DOORS OF HEAVEN

With one look in your eyes, you have touched the doors of heaven. You have raised the soul high beyond the clouds.

Once you've been lifted; one's desire is to be elevated again. It is a craving that is naturally enlightening, where warmness and tranquility come from every facet of emotion.

The spirit of light touches the soul and leads a passageway to the golden doors.

For God, He magnifies immense power by drawing all toward Him.

Within this great oracle, one experiences manifestations of mystical fusion that relieve many from pain, weariness, and despair.

Hitherto, and in all time, we can trust that we are his forever, for the goal of the Great One is to lead all devout hearts to the doors of heaven. Within them many will reside in His majestic presence for all eternity.

TRANQUIL

Simple, don't you think?

Why so complicated in this universe?

Oh, how delicate and radiant is the sunset, the breeze that wisps through the hair more beautiful than the human touch.

Alive is the warmth of the sun on the face. A warm summer's day beckons to flee from worries and just be.

Why, just there, adrift is a leaf, falling gently from the tree onto the ground.

Wind swiftly blows the pollinated flower petals, while bees fly to cultivate their honeycombs.

With outstretched arms, while lying in the grass lady bugs tickles the skin as they walk on them. Just a glance, nature is in motion all around Ants are constructing their intricate homesteads.

Soon it will be nightfall, as the sun too will close its eye, giving way to the light of the moon.

Now it is time to bid farewell on that great summer's day to creatures, nature high and low, just for now, until we come again tomorrow.

TRANSCEND AND GLORIOUS

Look up to the stars and be inspired by the King of kings. Fascination interlocks all with an essence of peace in the soul. Kneel and bow to the golden light raised above our heads.

Angelic ones dance merrily while in prayer.

High tidings and praises are given as a touch of the sun heats the cheeks of a babe, for his face is the closest to God.

In the body, a fluttering takes place as if butterflies are residing all over. The phenomenon is too intense for words to explicate it; even the mind is amazed and lured in by the greatest of light.

A charge takes over the soul to ignite electrical impulses, joining all of his children together and pouring in the spirit of eternal bliss and heavenly anointing.

UNEXPLAINED

Some say that in love one should not have to work hard; it should come easy. One could say that love is neither hard nor easy; it just is.

It is an emotional state that is excited by the biological releases of pheromones drawing in like magnetism. Human nature is what some call it.

It is a deepness of the soul controlled by the Holy Spirit; the Majestic One creates these feelings from the pure skies in heaven, and when we know, it leaves us inquisitive with ardent desire.

Once known, it is but a privilege and a welcomed longing; we would move any mountain, split the sea, and walk across desert lands in search of it—a quest to the ends of the earth.

Once found the treasure is to be cherished for all time. Unspeakable miracles occur in the bosom at insurmountable levels.

There are no measures or obstacles for the love that is true. It can be expressed by just looking into the eyes without speaking any words.

In the mind, man can dream of such a love with a hope that it exists. It is not in the form but quintessentially a joining of pure spirits in what could be described as love.

VOICES IN THE WIND

Temperatures reading below the Celsius mark from way up north.

Cold winter's wind has a humming of a familiar past; the frozen nose hairs tickle until you chuckle.

Is it the prince or princess who has forgotten? Or was it just a trick to fool a naïve heart?

Oh, what wonderment for the fooled one to fall for such trickery in this matter. The key was stolen to pull the wool over once again.

Now the door is locked, and the key is missing. Who has it? Many voices are humming in the wind.

As men and women reveal their faces, in their great bosoms they are filled like a Swiss Alps mountaintop.

The swirling of the cold air takes one's breath like the lover's kiss.

Even the ones who lack heart find heart in the tenderness of warm embraces. They too are in search of one who is true.

While waiting for that miracle, they fall to their knees to honor the Most High of love to grant them that missing key.

Perhaps the key to the door was there all along: love ourselves, and everything else will follow.

VITAL

Your very word flows freely like sap from a tree; the sound of your voice in my head is like the fluidity of water, so sweet is its tone that it contains the life of deliciousness.

Oh, how one who is weary yearns for more of wisdom to beautify the soul.

Smoothly, you swing death's door open and awaken the dark pit of the heart, fired up again like that of the legendary phoenix and left in squalor and misery.

Your power rings through and true, with such fierceness left unexplained. Brightly, from ashes, this gentle creature emerges with a vengeance, like no other—

Hidden from the world but revealed with just a flicker. You control all thoughts, all hands, all forms, and all minds. For the flicker that was silenced is now the everlasting phenomenon that many have yet to comprehend.

This great flicker is growing immensely above all who should know.

One lifts up with angel's wings that are risen higher than any soul can want to go, for the flicker, which is the phoenix, yearns to hear in all time the son of man's voice.

The sweetness of his words brings forth a glow that no man can mistake: He flickers His light within this very chest.

WALLS

The walls are witnesses of what lovers do.

They conceal all that is in the doing, for they know all the tender secrets and are loyal in every act.

The walls will never betray you; they are sealed like a kiss. The sacred walls hold the firsts of all lovers: first glance, first kiss, and first sensual embraces.

Ah, but within these walls is the quintessential desire—a mystery of elemental absorption of pure love contained within the cracks.

Why, the walls take on life itself and transform to something much more. Naturally they become alive in the element of the human spirit.

The aromas within the walls are intoxicating and intensify during the dance of love.

For love's precious moments allow for the joining of wonderful streams that flow freely, such passion floods and fills the rooms of lovers' havens every time.

For the walls that stand behind and around what is beautiful in life are timeless.

The natural things such as humidity are the aftereffect of temperatures risen above normal.

The walls transform and swell, but it is the never-ending acts that illuminate them when two bodies become one in love.

WATER

The reflection in the water is a stranger unknown to me—
The image is not too clear—recognizable, yet different in some way.
Although the water is transparent, at the same time it is murky, similar to that of the image.
In some way they are connected but through separate entities.
It could be that the water and the image are reflecting changes from within.
As we know, water assumes any form or shape, and reflected images become distorted. Unnatural things appear more comprehensible and concrete in this remarkable life liquid.
So impossible things are evolving into possibilities through a mystical realm from and within the image and water
Its natural source of power has been borrowed for a while now, controlling all things around it where images and water evolve into spirit. But how long will it last?
Mirages and daydreams toy with the mind in this water; it is hard to distinguish what is real or false.
At one area of the water, it is giving way to translucent fluidity. This signifies change in the greater sense because things become clear.
For the reflection of the water, one is looking inside of a new self being reborn into the light of God and His wondrous image in water, which is man.

WHERE?

Father, where am I today?

Why am I completely and utterly lost in yesterday?

As I dive into this dark ocean and hit the bottom, suddenly I am revived again, raised from the abyss, the water encompasses my form, and we are merged,

With great force, the currents twist me back and forth until I am on the shore—clothes drenched and wrung like a cloth, I am home again.

For this deepest part of me is awakened by my angel's voice. He says to me, why is it that you don't know where you are? You should know very well where you belong. Come hither to me, where you will dwell forever in the everlasting light

Suddenly, hands are around me; this water becomes tumultuous.

There is some darkness that sucks me in like a vacuum.

Once I felt free, but the great hands of some uncanny force would not let me be.

But behold, great warmth comes over me with a calming effect; such immense feelings and sensations brush against my flesh. Then an angel touches my waist gently.

Here I am, left on the shore, entangled with this smooth surface that feels like something familiar, a slight twist to my left, and I could not move.

Almost immediately my eyes opened, and in just a glance at my very form, I saw it was the bed sheets wrapping tightly around me once again.

How disappointing. I long for a life that once was.

It was only my sheets, not the human touch. It was just a dream—but how could that be?

Nevertheless, it was my room. This is where I dwell in reality.

YOU ARE HIS

Peer inside the doorway and find a pathway that waits, for the likeness in character is echoing in the wind, a powerful longing for yesterday. Familiar footsteps left an imprint that is permanent in the heart.

Gather your belongings and go on to the next if you dare, but you won't rest, for there is no other that exists such as you.

Marvel at your reflection, where the spirit of God's face dwells, put all your trust in him, but not in the opposite; it is on Him that one can rely, not on beings of artifice.

Devote your thoughts to his mind. The guide that you're seeking is his infinite light, for you are His only, and your likeness in character is His voice and no other.

YOUTH

The world is our youth

Empower them, encourage them with messages of love, and introduce them to the world when time is ready — not too soon, as a fruit is not ready to ripen.

Pace, operate gradually, for the workings of geniuses are among them. Pure as they are, lead them majestically, leaving them untouched, not tainted by man's faulty or artificial influence.

Study them not and set them free as birds do their suckling, place them atop a tree so that they can soar, mold them with infinite light of wisdom from above.

Natural knowledge is absorbed without words leaving the mouth; it seeps under the skin but into the heart's core.

Puzzling are the youth when puberty approaches, but before then, guide carefully. Let not the ill willed come near these gentle creatures of the future.

Why, they hold the secrets of tomorrow's world; they possess the keys to evolving knowledge.

Their light shapes the world when their hearts are pure. Hold close and witness what they can do.

Youth brings forth a new beginning—another dimension to the mind's eye.

Their great vision is set forth and is broken down in chapters of yesterday, today, and tomorrow.

REMINISCENCE

What is it in life that is joyous to reminisce about?

When times grow bleak, and I feel despair, I can whisper your name under my breath to secure all that is left of me.

I may ask myself: Is it all for nothing? Do I continue with this mockery of existence with this so-called merciless human race? Do they not witness the spirits that dance or dwell inside me? Do they wish to continue to use the ill forces to compel that which is benevolent?

Is destruction all we know? Did we not learn from those who succumbed to turbulent behavior?

But still, maybe there is hope for us all. Can we look to each other now and find peace?

I say NO! We cannot unless he dwells within us.

We can only look to Him for such answers, and he resides within the self—if you and I would only let him in.

He is forever and throughout all eternity the only answer to all life's questions.

WOMEN

We are God's gifts to men. Some may know it, some may not.
We possess absolute love that comes from above.
It is instilled in the nature, for women are the ones who facilitate life,
but without man, it is not possible, the Great One took one rib to create
man's image, which is the woman.
Nevertheless, each woman is uniquely and meticulously created.
Within is contained the embodiment of the light of love, for the Great
One has touched the soul to miraculously join man in woman as kin-
dred spirits.
This unification commences the birth of a new life.
Ignited in soul and spirit, both man and woman bear offspring when
the light and spirit of love is produced from two.

UNKNOWN

Go—walk toward your heart and remember the night in which you traveled in REM state, sleepless, listless, turning like wires coiled within a gate—

Twisted metal interlocking, resembling water because of its metallic shimmer

Bed sheets of satin tangles around the form too are familiar

Lying awake maybe, but not so,

In your sweat and angst one becomes a swimmer.

Thoughts in the mind ring louder than sirens from machines.

Whispers and murmurs of unfamiliar voices enter; a sudden sound arouses the deep sleep with a trumpeting sound of feet that leaves one in a quiver—

Journeying in the unconscious mystical world, not long, with just a tremor; the body begins to move about uncontrollably.

So remember, the unknown waits for the morrow to toil with man's might until the next sleeper searches for a good night.

THREE TIMES THE GRANDEUR

Faith comes in the third light and the sight of unseen occurrences.

Messengers sent through a channel of spiritual guidance from beings not of this earth look in the sky to find trails and a purpose that awaits the path to serve.

Look to the trees, they too are the makings from up above. Wind, whispering to the soul while footprints are forming before you—

Three times, the grandest of futuristic reminders of what is yet to come—

Diligence brings forth perseverance in days of plight and despair, discipline characterizes the tried and true, a glimpse to taunt and to straighten the path.

Senses embrace the unseen hands in the waking hour.

Warriors fall as the Great One did, but like him, the true warrior is resurrected for them to witness the great works.

Crown and knighted by him, three times lost hope, three times faith restored, three times the grandeur.

SAIL: EMPTY CONQUESTS

Conclude my life dear Father the sail is already directed to one's true destiny
Plans have been drawn out like coordinates on a map.
Open this chest and rip out the contents of the old to rebuild anew.
Flesh is painstakingly being mended for past present and future wounds,
The yearning of peace spill out in the blood, while the heart begins the restoration process.
Conquests are but empty wastes of precious time; solely the great one heals and transforms the spirit to a higher plane.
Levels are unimaginable for all to understand, for the Holy Spirit is tried in each way.
Prayer is the promise and the longing of an intimate closeness when we seek Him.
Hope strives towards a greatness that is delivered from perseverance.
Missing links are now being pieced together like a puzzle from where they belong
Miracles in the world allow for communication through the mind without speaking a word. But are spirits out of touch? Though they are far, still all are connected, and the universe has joined all missing links.
Nay, they travel the earth toward the familiar.
Spirits are no longer wandering aimlessly searching for a missing link.
All things come to pass and have their day in a season.
Follow the heart, for it knows the way to the spirit and soul.
It directs the mind; both are interlocked like the fabric of time.

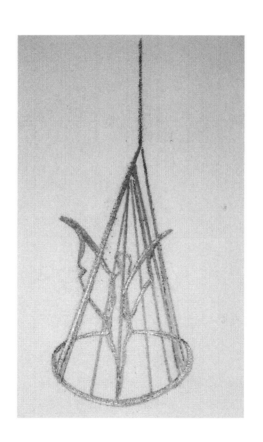

ABOUT THE AUTHOR

Lisa Alexander was born in the Bronx, New York, and raised in Queens.

She earned an Associates Degree in Liberal Arts at Touro College NYSCAS, and a Bachelors Degree in Studio Art from York College, City University of New York.

Real life experiences inspire her writing.

Made in the USA
Columbia, SC
16 December 2018